Remain

50 Devotions to Abide Like You Belong

Tara Smith

WestBow
PRESS®
A DIVISION OF THOMAS NELSON
& ZONDERVAN

NIV: All Scripture quotations, unless otherwise indicated, are taken from the Holy
Bible, New International Version®, NIV®. Copyright ©1973, 1978, 1984, 2011 by
Biblica, Inc.™ Used by permission of Zondervan. All rights reserved worldwide.
www.zondervan.com The "NIV" and "New International Version" are trademarks
registered in the United States Patent and Trademark Office by Biblica, Inc.

ESV: Scripture quotations are from the ESV® Bible (The Holy Bible, English
Standard Version®), copyright © 2001 by Crossway, a publishing ministry
of Good News Publishers. Used by permission. All rights reserved.

WestBow Press books may be ordered through booksellers or by contacting:

WestBow Press
A Division of Thomas Nelson & Zondervan
1663 Liberty Drive
Bloomington, IN 47403
www.westbowpress.com
1 (866) 928-1240

Because of the dynamic nature of the Internet, any web addresses or links contained in
this book may have changed since publication and may no longer be valid. The views
expressed in this work are solely those of the author and do not necessarily reflect the
views of the publisher, and the publisher hereby disclaims any responsibility for them.

Any people depicted in stock imagery provided by Getty Images are models,
and such images are being used for illustrative purposes only.
Certain stock imagery © Getty Images.

Quote pages hand lettered by Paris Erwin.

ISBN: 978-1-9736-5006-5 (sc)
ISBN: 978-1-9736-5007-2 (hc)
ISBN: 978-1-9736-5005-8 (e)

Library of Congress Control Number: 2018915177

Print information available on the last page.

WestBow Press rev. date: 5/30/2019

Acknowledgments

$\mathcal{I}$ dedicate this work of heart to the family and friends who saw a writer in me before I ever noticed it in myself. To all the people who pushed and encouraged me to keep writing —thank you! To my husband and kids who love me well and teach me every day what a gift it is to be a mom and wife—your love and support humble me in so many ways.

To my God who has redeemed me and grown me and is constantly reminding me of my worth—I'm your girl. Thank you for creating me with gifts and talents through which I can bless others. Thank you for healing all the hurt places in me so that I can be slightly less of a hot mess. Thank you for allowing me to use my story to encourage other women.

To all the #bossbabes out there who keep showing up and using your big hearts to change the world—thank you. You've inspired me to dream big, show up in my own life, and push through the obstacles along the way.

Love you big,
Tara

A Note from Tara

Hey friend! I'm just going to go ahead and call you that now, because in this little devotional we'll go deep, fast. As I dreamed up and prayed over this book, I got this image in my mind of women everywhere curled up with their morning coffee meeting Jesus through the words on these pages. It still gives me chills every time that image comes to mind, and it has been the thing that keeps me going through the process of writing. These entries are honest and straight from the heart.

Oxford Dictionary defines the word remain as follows: continuing to exist, especially after other similar or related people or things have ceased to exist. The Bible's use of remain suggests a devoted, consistent and reliant "staying". John 15:4 says, "Remain in me, and I will remain in you. For a branch cannot produce fruit if it is severed from the vine, and you cannot be fruitful unless you remain in me."- John15:4 (NLT).

May we learn together to remain in Him as we face trials and circumstances of many kinds. It is my heart's desire that this book leaves you a little more encouraged, a little more empowered and a lot more in love with the identity your creator has written over you. Let's abide like we belong, friend.

Xoxo,
Tara

"Remain in me, and I will remain in you. For a branch cannot produce fruit if it is severed from the vine, and you cannot be fruitful unless you remain in me."-John15:4 (NLT)

Contents

comparison is the thief of joy

THEODORE ROOSEVELT

Comparison

"Am I now trying to win the approval of human beings, or of God? Or am I trying to please people? If I were still trying to please people, I would not be a servant of Christ."- Galatians 1:10

"Let your eyes look straight ahead; fix your gaze directly before you. Give careful thought to the paths for your feet and be steadfast in all your ways." -Proverbs 4:25-26

Theodore Roosevelt coined the increasingly popular phrase, "Comparison is the thief of joy." I couldn't agree more. Comparison demolishes relationships and stunts growth. I'll admit I have personally shown some serious ugly in a state of comparison. The trickiest part about it all is that our intentions are typically good. We want to be a better mom, wife, homemaker, friend, etc. So, we look around and we start to compare our lives. But instead of getting inspired and encouraged to rise up and be what God has called us to be in these areas, we obsess over the canyon sized chasm we see between our life and the lives of women we admire who are doing these things well. Our good intentions of growth quickly transform into a twisted victim mindset.

That's just what Satan would want of us, isn't it? —to spend so much time worried about how we measure up to other women that we have no time to build one another up or do great things for the kingdom. The devil is so discrete and so insidious in that way. When we take our eyes off of our Creator, our minds and hearts automatically turn inward. When we open our minds to self-doubt and comparison, we are giving the devil a foothold in our thought lives.

John 15:16 says we have been CHOSEN and appointed by God to bear fruit. Nowhere in there does it say that we've been chosen to bear fruit only if someone else hasn't already produced that type of fruit or only if we're feeling comfortable and capable of the whole fruit-bearing process. It's as if we are saying, "Sorry God, I'm not feeling like you did a good enough job on me, so I'm just going to sit back and sulk while other women change the world." He didn't ask if we'd be good enough to bear fruit. He says that we were made "enough" when He created us and that we need to stop walking backwards through life trying to get ahead to something we have had all along.

Pray with me: *Lord, know my heart and mind. Help me to recognize when I am comparing myself to someone else or even to different versions of myself. Help me to believe that You saying I'm enough is all that I need to be enough. Help me to live loved and to be outwardly focused. Allow me to take my eyes off of myself so that I can see the needs of others around me and celebrate the women in my life. I pray against Satan's schemes to try to tempt me into self-pity and victimization. You are my protector and my source of peace. In your great name I say, Amen.*

Notes

A Call to Transparency

"As a prisoner for the Lord, then, I urge you to live a life worthy of the calling you have received. Be completely humble and gentle; be patient, bearing with one another in love. Make every effort to keep the unity of the Spirit through the bond of peace."
Ephesians 4:1-3

"Therefore, each of you must put off falsehood and speak truthfully to your neighbor, for we are all members of one body."
-Ephesians 4:25

Let's be real for a minute, can we? In recent times I have been relieved to see a small movement of women who are willing to be more honest about life and their portrayal of it, especially in the realm of social media. But, in large part, our world is still very much full of people who are parading behind masks of perfection. It's funny and sad if you think about the paradox of it all. Some spend so much time and energy trying to appear flawless, but I'm guessing if I sat down with these people they would eventually admit how exhausting and frustrating it feels to constantly be portraying perfection while still not feeling fulfilled or adequate. In truth, the people creating the standard don't even measure up to the standard or even realize they're feeding into the standard at all for that matter.

On the other side, there are the people who believe the perfection being portrayed is authentic. I'm not sure which is a scarier place to reside. I have fallen into that trap a time or two while scrolling Instagram and swooning over beautifully curated photos of designer homes and perfectly dressed moms with their neatly groomed children. Oh, how dangerous that can be. We have to realize that we are all one and the same. We're all women created and loved by God. He is the only one able to achieve perfection and He should be our standard of it. These earthly standards we're chasing are preventing us from entering into the real and raw conversations and relationships that our hearts desire.

Vulnerability gives people the permission to let their guard down. If we can just get honest with ourselves and with others, I think we'd soon experience some major freedom and connection. When we are transparent with others, they feel comfortable being transparent in return. This is how we can share in one another's burdens and joys. This is how we have true relationship— the kind Jesus modeled for us. I don't know about you, but I'm totally ok with living with that as my standard. I mean, Jesus had a pretty good track record in the whole "loving people well and being relational" department.

So, let's commit to being more real. Let's stop putting on a facade to please others or save face. In doing so we will invite others to do the same. What freedom we'd all experience simply from being unapologetically ourselves. How much more energy we would have to put toward being thoughtful and considerate of others when it's not being spent on comparing or pretending.

Pray with me: *Lord, thank you for the women in our lives who are living real. Thank you for what your word teaches us about loving one another and loving ourselves. Help us to live in a state of transparency. Let us be open to entering into the lives of others. Make us brave in using the pain of our journey to minister to others. Let our conversations be filled with truth and grace, always bringing you glory. Amen.*

Notes

Worry Wart

"Do not be anxious about anything, but in every situation, by prayer and petition, with thanksgiving, present your requests to God. And the peace of God, which transcends all understanding, will guard your hearts and your minds in Christ Jesus."
Philippians 4:6-7

If you knew me growing up, you'd know I was the poster child for worry. I mean from a very early age I was anxious over way too many things. I was nervous about riding in a car over an overpass for crying out loud! I definitely had some circumstances surrounding my childhood that may have led me to worry much more than other kids my age, but it carried on through my adult years too.

For many years it plagued me—through high school and college, and maybe most of all, once I became a mom. All you mamas out there surely know what I mean. You mean I have a whole other person to worry over now?! *Cue helicopter mom even though I promised I would never be her. * Anyway, it kept me from truly trusting God and living my best life. In the past couple of years, I became more determined than ever to get it under control. I fell short time after time trying to muster up enough courage to not struggle with it. It wasn't until I began to practice the act of surrendering my mind daily and completely to the Lord that I finally felt worry loosen its ugly grip on me.

About a year ago someone brought four words to my attention and I haven't forgotten them since. I have claimed Philippians 4:6-10 as my life verse for many years now. I have written it a billion times, posted it all over my house, committed it to memory, given it out to others for encouragement—but for some reason have never noticed the four words that come right before it. It's a prerequisite to this passage I have loved for so long, and I hadn't ever given it any attention. At the end of verse five it says, "The Lord is near." BOOM—mind blown. Because the Lord is near you don't have to worry. Because the Lord is near you don't have to be anxious about anything. Because He is with you, you can simply hand over those anxious thoughts and what ifs and fears and be comforted by the one who created you.

In hindsight, it makes sense that I had such tunnel vision on the action part of the passage. I kept thinking, I just need to get over myself and do it already, when in reality He wanted me to stop in my tracks and simply give it up. Isn't worry such a funny thing? It's this false sense of control when we feel out of control. For some ironic reason we think that obsessing over it will make it better. So, we run ourselves into the ground circling the issue at hand with our what ifs, our maybes and our if-thens instead of circling it in prayer. All along, He's watching us and waiting for us to just quit it already and lean in to Him. He created us to need Him and we actually bring Him glory when we allow Him to work that out in our lives.

Pray with me: *God, thank you that you are the lifter of my head and the protector of my heart. Help me to be aware of the times when I am allowing worry and anxiety to creep in and give me false "security". Help me in those moments to choose to put my eyes on you and surrender instead of giving in to those anxious thoughts. I know that you are the Prince of Peace and oh, how I crave just that. Cover me in your perfect peace as I go about my day. Amen!*

Notes

you
cannot pour
from an
empty cup

The Empty Cup

*"May the God of hope fill you with all joy and
peace as you trust in him, so that you may overflow
with hope by the power of the Holy Spirit."
-Romans 15:13*

I was driving on my way to church and from the back seat I hear, "Mommy, do you need to stop and fill up your car?" My inquisitive girl noticed the gas station we were passing and thought she might give her forgetful Mama a reminder. What I took from it was a bit deeper. Back up to before we left the house that morning. My husband is a pastor so I'm on my own on Sunday mornings as far as getting everyone ready, fed, and out the door. This morning my sweet "P" was on a mission to have a showdown over brushing her teeth. *And all the mamas give a knowing nod.* After asking her 247 times to brush her teeth while doing five other things at the same time, I lost it. I yelled, I spanked, I blamed her for making us late.

I feel pretty small admitting that. I don't believe in that sort of parenting at all. It's never productive. She was upset, I was upset, and little brother was crying for sympathetic support. I felt like a big ol' mess. I got down and apologized, she apologized and we all hugged and prayed Jesus would change our "yucky attitudes". So, instead of a question about getting gas in the car I heard "Mommy, do you need to stop and fill your cup?" Although we had already made amends, God was showing me I was obviously trying to pour from an empty cup. My husband was leaving that day after church for six days, we were packing our house to move, I was going to be left trying to figure out any repairs that needed to be done, etc.

Sometimes, the perfect storm happens, and we lose it. But, what if we could catch it before it ever got to that point? I had spent time in the word that morning, but I hadn't brought all my worries and anxious thoughts before the Lord. I hadn't allowed His perfect peace to wash over me. When we feel those thoughts in the back of our mind start to control our reactions, we need to stop in our tracks and shed light on them with the only One that can tame those waves. If I had done so earlier that morning, I wouldn't have lost it with my daughter. I would have taken time to bend down and explain what I needed from her or pretended that brushing your teeth is some cool game where you can get an imaginary prize (Hey, that works for four year olds...sometimes).

The point is, we can't pour from an empty cup. We also can't keep from pouring out. We have responsibilities all throughout our day that require us to pour out bits of ourselves, our time, our energy. We have got to be filled up in order to pour out goodness and holiness and self-control. Yes, it takes conscious effort. But, I'd rather put the effort there than in apologizing for being "Mean Mommy".

Pray with me: Father, you know me. You know what worries me and irritates me and scares me. You also know that I have good intentions, but sometimes fail miserably because I try to do it all in my own power. Help me to be more preventative by meeting with you each morning and giving you whatever is troubling me. Fill me up, so that I can pour out goodness and gentleness. I believe this is what you want for me and I believe that I CAN live a FULL life. Amen!

Notes

Are You a Joy Girl?

"May the God of hope fill you with all joy and peace as you trust in him, so that you may overflow with hope by the power of the Holy Spirit."-Romans 15:13 (NIV)

"Joy is the settled assurance that God is in control of all the details of my life, the quiet confidence that ultimately everything is going to be all right, and the determined choice to praise God in all things." -Kay Warren

It took me awhile to realize joy and happiness are not the same thing. Happiness is an emotion we feel when things are going well. It is lovely, but also circumstantial and fleeting.

Joy on the other hand is something we choose. It isn't based on the circumstance we are facing. In fact, we are often in the midst of trial when we are called to choose joy.

It's not that we're called to put on a happy face and pretend everything is alright. It's a state of surrender where we recognize Jesus as Lord over our life and trust in His sovereignty over all things. As we release control we make room in our hearts and minds to praise. When our focus turns from worry to praise, we can choose to see the good in our lives and the ways God has blessed us—we can choose joy.

Whatever you are walking through right now, whether it's an earth-shattering sorrow, a mountain top high, or the daily mundane—you have the choice. You can choose to let life happen "to" you, being tossed about in the circumstantial waves of life OR you can choose to open your hands and heart to what the Lord wants for you in this season. You can choose joy. If you're anything like me, you need this written in 57 different places so that as soon as you forget it you see it again. Write it down, post it everywhere, tell it to a friend. You were made to be a joy girl—claim it!

Pray with me: *Lord, choosing joy is HARD sometimes! Some days it's all I can do to just get through the day with the stress and the weight of what I'm experiencing. Lord, when I am in the midst of those moments where it feels like I can only survive, remind me that you call me to greater things. You call me to choose surrender, because that's what's best for me. Help me to surrender in those moments and to thrive through those circumstances by choosing praise and joy. I trust that you can supply my every need and change my heart when need be. Thank you for being my all in all. Amen!*

Notes

_____

_____

_____

_____

_____

_____

_____

_____

_____

_____

_____

_____

_____

_____

_____

I praise you
FOR I AM
fearfully
AND
wonderfully
made

PSALM 139:14

Body Image

*"For you created my inmost being; you knit me together in
my mother's womb. I praise you because I am fearfully and
wonderfully made; your works are wonderful, I know that full well.
My frame was not hidden from you when I was made in the secret
place, when I was woven together in the depths of the earth. Your
eyes saw my unformed body; all the days ordained for me were
written in your book before one of them came to be. How precious
to me are your thoughts, God. How vast is the sum of them!"*
-Psalm 139:13-17

Let's talk body image for a second. I feel like I can guess pretty accurately that you've struggled with it at some point in your life. Whether you have been underweight, overweight, or just have something about your body that you don't love, we all struggle in some way or another. I get it. My post baby bod definitely isn't what it used to be. It's one thing to work toward the goal of being healthy and caring for your body in a way that makes it possible to show up in all the ways you've been called to. It's another thing to allow body image to consume you. When our mind fixates on something and we end up spending countless minutes (or hours) a day thinking about it and putting efforts in to conceal or change it, that, my friend, has become an idol.

Webster's defines an "idol" as an image or representation of a God that is used as an object of worship. I know, it feels weird to think that worrying about how we look could be a form of worship or idolatry in our lives, but that's just what it is, and we must not downplay the gravity of that. When we take a created thing and make it a pinnacle thing, we've got an idol. I think the hardest part about realizing that obsessing over body image is an idol is the fact that it's not just about looks. It runs deeper. For many of us, our appearance is tied strongly to our identity. Although that might not be the truth, it is a reality for so many women. If they don't feel beautiful, then they don't feel worthy.

Let me share with you a sobering question I ask myself when I start to slip into the trap of insecurity: How does God feel about me calling His creation unworthy or not enough? We are the ones putting those labels on ourselves. Yes, others might say them or allude to them, but we are the ones who decide if those things stick to us. We are the ones who decide whether the world or our Creator defines us. It's us, ladies. Let's be the example for every woman around us today—our family, our friends, and especially our daughters. Choose to love your body, your personality, your quirks. After all, they were made by a perfect God who doesn't make mistakes.

Pray with me: *Lord, you created us and know every intricate detail of who we are. The Bible says we are made in your very image. On the days where we feel less than and struggle to see our worth, remind us. Remind us that we are yours and we are loved. Forgive us for calling your creation anything less than fearfully and wonderfully made. Help us grow in a holy kind of self-love. Amen.*

Notes

Boundaries

*"Above all else, guard your heart, for
everything you do flows from it."*
-Proverbs 4:23

*"Scripture is full of admonitions to separate ourselves
from people who act in destructive ways. We are not
being unloving. Separating ourselves protects love,
because we are taking a stand against things that destroy
love." -John Townsend & Henry Cloud (Boundaries)*

Something that God has taught me over time is that boundaries are necessary for healthy relationships. Boundaries are not intended to keep people out. They are intended to keep us healthy. We need them at work, we need them at home, we need them in our thought life—we need them pretty much everywhere. Consider a child for instance. Boundaries are created by parents to keep them safe, healthy and thriving. It's easy to draw up boundaries for others, but not as simple for ourselves.

Early in our marriage, my husband and I went to counseling. (Which I highly suggest for EVERY marriage.) We were having a difficult time communicating and resolving conflict and it helped tremendously. One of the things I discovered about myself during that time was that I was acting slightly codependent in our marriage. If Moe came home with a bad attitude from something that had happened at work, I took that on. Even if I had a great day and was feeling positive, I allowed his negative emotion to control my emotions and consequently the rest of the night in our home. I took on his burden, but not in a healthy way.

I have had to learn over time the difference between entering into someone's pain and circumstances out of compassion versus taking on their burdens as my own. When Moe comes home in an angry huff, I have a boundary now (that has taken a lot of practice might I add). I give him some space to cool off and then I enter in and see if he's ready to talk about it. I don't take it personally, because it's not.

If you are a workaholic, maybe your first boundary project needs to be at work. Are you saying yes to please? Are you taking on more than is healthy because someone wants you to or to maintain a desired image? Do you need to practice saying "no" more often? It is not selfish to evaluate your actions—it's completely necessary if you want to live a balanced life. Another area of struggle might be with extended family relationships.

I have a good friend who was experiencing tension at almost every family gathering she attended, because she constantly felt left out and belittled by one of her husband's family members. She wanted so badly to have a good relationship with this person, which was a noble effort. However, because the other person has a toxic personality that thrives on drama, my dear friend had to come to a realization that the relationship she had been attempting to build was always going to be one sided. A boundary line had to be drawn. She decided that she would always be cordial and accommodating in a healthy way, but she would no longer seek to make a deeper connection with the person. She was no longer going to let a sideways comment or an irritable attitude from this person affect the time she had at a family gathering. What victory!

Boundaries are a form of self-care that we all need to practice. In what area(s) or with whom do you struggle to have boundaries? Take a minute to reflect on that. What boundary lines might you need to draw in these places or relationships? Be intentional about making a plan. Boundaries are not going to feel comfortable at first, but I promise you they will offer the kind of freedom and balance in your relationships that your heart is longing for. When you assert your boundaries, people may not like it at first, but they will respect it. Let's pray for some boundary making courage this week!

Pray with me: *Lord, you know where I struggle. You know where I lack the assertiveness or courage to draw a boundary line. Reveal to me today where these areas are. Help me to make a plan for placing boundaries so that I can live in the kind of freedom you intended for me. I want to love my people well, and to do that I need the balance of the peace you offer. Be with me in this, Jesus. Amen.*

Notes

_____

_____

_____

_____

_____

_____

_____

_____

_____

_____

_____

_____

_____

_____

Choosing Your Tribe

"Whoever walks with the wise will become wise;
whoever walks with fools will suffer harm."
- Proverbs 13:20 (NIV)

"So, encourage each other and build each other
up, just as you are already doing."
-1 Thessalonians 5:11 (NIV)

My husband is a youth pastor and before our kids came on the scene I spent a lot of time helping lead teen girls in the youth group. Something I heard my husband preach over and over again like a broken record was that you are who you surround yourself with. It's not that he didn't have any other good material, they just needed to hear it repeatedly. When I started writing this entry, I feared it might feel a little juvenile. After some thought though, I don't believe this message is just for young women. This is for everyone. I see women of all ages strive to impress and adapt to people around them so that they can feel accepted and part of something, even if that means compromising who they are.

I love community and I love lots of different people from lots of different walks of life. I would never detour someone from creating a relationship with anyone. Relationships are how Christ operated his ministry and He hardwired us with a need for them. They're extremely important to making others feel loved and cared for. If there is no relationship, then how would someone be led to the kingdom? The importance of relationship is not at question here. The focus here is that the people we spend the majority of our time with, the people we seek advice from, the people we lean on when times are difficult—those people need to line up with what we believe. If we are not seeking like-minded friends in the times we need accountability and to be pointed to the truth, these friends have the capability to sway our thinking in a way that isn't healthy. Not that they would intend to do so—they just live by different standards and have different convictions.

Choose your tribe wisely. Be around the sort of people you want to be more like. Like it or not, the people you spend time with will inevitably rub off on you. Spend time with the people who encourage and lift you up. If you're in a place where you don't feel you have many solid friends, pray for that! What is more God honoring than a couple of Jesus' girls coming together? Of course God would grant that desire. In the meantime, focus on being the kind of friend you desire.

Pray with me: *Jesus, you know me, and you know my desire for healthy relationships. You created me to be connected with people. Lord, help me to establish healthy relationships and strengthen the ones you have already placed in my life. Help me to be the kind of friend my friends need. Keep my ears open to your voice and how you want to use me to speak life into the people in my sphere of influence. Guide me in establishing boundaries in the friendships that may not line up with your best plan for me. Forgive me for any ways I have traded your best for me for circumstantial acceptance. I trust you in this area of my life and I surrender to you any worry. Amen!*

Notes

God is
NOT
the author
of
confusion

1 CORINTHIANS 14:33

Confusion

"For I know the plans I have for you," declares the Lord, "plans to prosper you and not to harm you, plans to give you hope and a future." -Jeremiah 29:11

"For God is not the author of confusion, but of peace, as in all churches of the saints."
-1 Corinthians 14:33 (KJV)

I was 19 years old and I had a decision to make. I was attending a university in Southern California and had just returned from an amazing study abroad experience in Spain. I needed to decide if I was going to head back to my current school for the remainder of my college career or take an opportunity to live somewhere I had never even visited before—Bozeman, Montana. In the spirit of adventure, I was excited about the move. I had this gut feeling like something good would happen there. But, the comfort of all I knew (plus the beaches and sunny weather of San Diego) made me extremely apprehensive about making a change.

With an enrollment deadline looming right around the corner, I could not for the life of me make a decision. I talked to friends and family, thoroughly researched both options, and prayed like nobody's business. One day I was talking with my mom and she told me, "Honey, God is not the author of confusion." This war within me about making a "right" choice wasn't from Him. The opportunity was from Him. I finally realized that maybe there wasn't a "right" choice. When we are in a season where we have to make a decision, we should: offer it up in prayer, seek wise counsel, and then TRUST. We trust that whatever we choose, God will be in it with us. We trust that He is the one in control and that He will close the doors He doesn't want us walking through. If we are coming to Him with our requests and aligning our lives with what we know is good and true, then we really can't make a "wrong" decision.

If you're curious, I ended up taking the opportunity. I packed up my life and my best friend and I moved to Montana. In the two years I lived there, I experienced a little bit of every emotion. There were times of great joy and times of loneliness. Most of all though, there was GROWTH beyond measure. God did something in me when I trusted Him with that big decision. He did something in me while I experienced adversity there. He matured me and taught me what it meant to live in community with believers and non-believers. He taught me how to seek Him daily. He used people, and circumstances, and those breathtaking mountain views to change me forever. I'll always remember my Bozeman days with fondness and I'll always be grateful I took the opportunity to jump even when it felt scary.

Are you in a season where you have a decision to make? Let me encourage you to first pray. Seeking wise counsel is very helpful and biblical, but make sure you first consult the one who has already written your story. He knows what we will decide and how He will walk through it with us. He has the very best plans for us and desires that we trust Him completely in carrying out those plans. Take that leap of faith and watch how He works.

Pray with me: *Lord, you are the great author—the writer of our stories. Help us to trust that you always have what is best for us. When we find ourselves at a crossroad, teach us to pray through it. Overwhelm us with your perfect peace in those moments. Go before us and prepare a way for our future. Thank you that your plans are always good. Amen.*

Notes

Empowered to Empower

*"Therefore encourage one another and build
one another up, just as you are doing."
- 1 Thessalonians 5:11 (ESV)*

*"Two are better than one, because they have a good
reward for their toil. For if they fall, one will lift up his
fellow. But woe to him who is alone when he falls and has
not another to lift him up!"-Ecclesiastes 4:9-10 (ESV)*

There's nothing I love more than seeing women empower other women. It's so motivating and inspiring and against the grain of what the world does. Being a wife is hard, being a mom is hard, being a woman in general can be hard. The last thing we need is for someone to make it harder by criticizing or judging our efforts. When we cut one another down and choose gossip or judgment over working through conflict or celebrating one another's accomplishments, we are sabotaging far more than we know.

We are hardwired for relationship and I believe wholeheartedly that God uses people to work out His plans. I don't know how many times God has used a friend or mentor to speak truth and encouragement into my weary soul at just the right time. Before I ever led a Bible study, it was a leader on a mission trip that told me she could see me leading. Before I ever saw myself teaching, it was my husband who told me he could see me being a teacher. Before ever entertaining the idea of writing a book, it was a friend who affirmed my gift of writing and told me I should write a book. It's not that I needed the permission to do these things. But, because someone important to me saw traits in me I couldn't see myself and was willing to speak them to me, I then began to believe those things too.

We need people. We need to be "those" people. We set the tone for the sort of people we attract into our lives. When we are speaking well of others and lifting one another up, it's contagious. When someone feels lifted up, they are more confident. When people feel confident, they are more likely to find themselves encouraging and lifting up others. Imagine the chain reaction we could ignite if we were all focused on empowerment.

It's not always natural though. I wake up many days focused on how tired I am and overwhelmed with my to-do list for the day. When we are focused on ourselves, we don't usually consider others. That's why it's so important to begin our days with the Lord. When we start our day coming before Him and laying down our stress and our weariness, He gives us the power to do more than just persevere. In His power, we can push past personal survival mode and pour into the lives of others. In His power, we can encourage and build up. In His power, we can overcome the temptation to be threatened by women around us when they succeed and rather celebrate with them. In His power, we can be living proof to the world that He exists and is present in our everyday.

Pray with me: *Jesus, thank you for the people you've placed in my life that support and love me. Thank you for the ways you use us to build one another up. What a cool design. Please help me to be that for others. Help me to have an outward focus when I go throughout my day, so that I can be aware of the needs of others. Help me to be sensitive to your voice nudging me to do or say things that will build someone up. Amen.*

Notes

_____

_____

_____

_____

_____

_____

_____

_____

_____

_____

_____

_____

_____

_____

_____

Brave Girl

"That is why, for Christ's sake, I delight in weaknesses,
in insults, in hardships, in persecutions, in difficulties.
For when I am weak, then I am strong."
-2 Corinthians 12:10

"Not only so, but we also glory in our sufferings, because we
know that suffering produces perseverance; perseverance,
character; and character, hope. And hope does not put us to
shame, because God's love has been poured out into our hearts
through the Holy Spirit, who has been given to us."-Romans 5:3-5

*W*hen I hear the word brave, I think of my friend Salem. She is a feisty and full of life 30-year-old with a heart for broken women. In 2015, she entered a Haitian brothel and was overcome with compassion for the women there. This experience led her to move to Haiti full-time and create a non-profit called New Life Campaign. New Life Campaign is an organization that works with broken, abused, and sexually exploited women. I read some of her posts and I honestly wonder how she does it—the heartbreak, the third world struggles, the uncertainty of day to day life. I just couldn't imagine. SHE is brave.

The funny thing is though, if you were to ask her about it she would most likely deny that attribute. So it goes with people who reflect bravery the most, right? She is fiercely passionate about these women she serves. She pours herself into her ministry so selflessly and depends on the Lord so desperately that she forgets she's being brave. She is honest and real about her struggles though, and that's what I adore about her.

She recently posted this, and I couldn't help but share. "But you were made to be this brave little human who does not back down to the things in life that try to tidal wave over you and force you to be small. I'm letting you know it's ok to feel weak and worn and have days that tidal wave over you. But know that you are not small. You are brave. You are seen. You are known. And you are understood. The enemy can never snuff out that light. So, let's tell him to kick rocks." Don't you love her?!

Salem reminds me that it's not about being "brave". It's about committing to live the call we've been given with determination and complete dependence. When we do that, we end up living brave. But first, it takes a yes—a surrender of our will to one that is far greater than us. Wherever you are in life (motherhood, corporate world, missions, ministry, education) and whatever mountain you are facing, you've got this girl! Don't worry about trying to get there and be some other person. Don't try to pretend it's not a struggle. Get honest with yourself, lay it in the hands of the God who loves you, and then put your big girl pants on because it's going to be a wild ride. God called YOU and so you are the one He wants to do this—feeling brave or not.

Pray with me: Lord, you are the author of brave. You don't require us to feel fearless when you call us. In fact, you want us to be honest about our weakness and frailty, because that leaves room for your power to come in and swoop us up. You know what I'm facing in my life right now. Maybe it's not a third world tragedy, but it's big to me nonetheless. I surrender this to you, Lord, and I ask you to be my courage. Be my strength on the days I can't do it one more second. Be my hope. Be my all in all. Thank you that you hear me and love me in a way that completes me. You make me brave. In Jesus' precious name, Amen.

Notes

_____

_____

_____

_____

_____

_____

_____

_____

_____

_____

_____

_____

_____

_____

_____

HE

makes us

ENOUGH

Enough

"Therefore, if anyone is in Christ, he is a new creation. The old has passed away; behold, the new has come." -2 Corinthians 5:17 (ESV)

"The word of the LORD came to me, saying, Before I formed you in the womb I knew you, before you were born I set you apart; I appointed you as a prophet to the nations." -Jeremiah 1:4-5

I was talking to a friend the other day who was going through a really trying time. She and her husband had recently felt called to move their family to a different state and pursue something kind of scary and totally God honoring. The weekend before her move, two different friends called in crisis, her family car broke down and she learned their new town was literally on fire. Talk about some serious spiritual attacks! She started to question whether or not they were really supposed to move and even more she started to question her capability to fill her new position. She told me, "Tara, I just don't know if I'm spiritual enough to do this. I've cussed more in the last week than in our whole 10 years of marriage." Isn't she cute?

When God calls us to something, He does not expect us to come "enough". He is calling us because He knows exactly what He has designed in us and because we are a perfect match for what He's looking for. He expects us to simply say yes and allow Him to do the rest. Look at some of the heroes of the Bible who did brave and amazing things for the kingdom. Not one of them started out that way.

Paul was a Christian hater. Moses was an angry and insecure boy with a speech impediment. Esther was a poor orphan. The list goes on and on. The passage surrounding the Jeremiah verse above is so good, friend. God is calling Jeremiah to go and prophecy to the nations during the Babylonian exile. Basically, he is supposed to warn the people that judgement is coming for them. Of course, Jeremiah immediately questions his capability to do what God asks. God quiets his doubt with the verse above and he goes on to tell him that He will be with him and rescue him no matter what. This promise stands for us as well.

No one can be spiritual enough, strong enough, or brave enough on their own. It's all Him. We are simply vessels through which He chooses to accomplish His will, and what an honor it is. So, let's shift our focus from "what if" to "watch this". Watch as God works in your heart and mind. Watch where He takes you as you submit and trust Him. Watch as the old habits and hang ups fall off and the new takes hold. You don't need years of preparation, you just need a "yes".

Pray with me: *Lord, your word says that we are a new creation in you. Thank you that you see past what we've done and who we've been to who we will be. Remind us daily that it's a life of dependence and surrender that accomplishes your will, not fancy words or spiritual stature. Jesus thank you for your sacrifice so that we might live a life in such connection to you. What a blessing that is. Amen.*

Notes

Expectations

"Jesus Christ is the same yesterday and today and forever."
-Hebrews 13:8

*"Every good and perfect gift is from above, coming
down from the Father of the heavenly lights, who
does not change like shifting shadows."*
-James 1:17

While my husband and I were engaged, we went through premarital counseling. I'll always remember the night our mentors explained to us how important it is to recognize and communicate expectations in order to prevent conflict and live harmoniously together. We hadn't really thought about that before, but we learned quickly exactly what they meant. Take our first married Valentine's Day for example. I woke up so giddy. What things could he have planned for us? Would he surprise me and bring flowers by my work? Would he write a sweet card expressing his love for me? I got ready while he was still asleep and placed the card and gift I had been working on for weeks on the dining room table. I had written him 50 things I loved about him on these cute little papers and decorated a mason jar with photos of us to house them in. Maybe you can already see where this is going.

After placing my gifts on the table, I walked around the house and didn't notice anything for myself, so I figured he must be planning something for later on. I kissed him goodbye and headed off to work. The day went by and let me tell you, there were no cards, no flowers, no dinner plans—nothing. I was heartbroken. When I got home I confronted him in tears. He had no idea I had built this up in my head and he was completely defensive about being held to these expectations. I didn't even realize they were expectations. I just considered these things common practice in a marriage. I had unknowingly set myself up for disappointment. Expectations almost always end in heartbreak.

Whether we know where they come from or not, we all have them. Because of that, I'm sure that someone in your life has let you down at some point. Every single one of us has been let down and we all let people down. Why? Because we are HUMAN! Anytime we put our hope in someone other than Jesus, we *will* be disappointed. He is the only true constant and the only one big enough and perfect enough to never let us down. Take a minute today to write down some expectations you've been holding onto. Consider how letting go of those expectations could change your relationships.

Pray with me: *Lord, you are my constant. I praise you for you are always good! You are my provider, my strength, and my peace. Reveal to me the expectations I've been holding on to. Help me to release those things and consequently let some of the people in my life off the hook. Remind me that you are the only one that can provide for me and fill me fully. Help me to be more dependent on you in this area of my life. In Jesus' name, Amen.*

Notes

forgiveness

IS A

freedom

THING

~‿~

Forgiveness

*"And do not grieve the Holy Spirit of God, with whom you
were sealed for the day of redemption. Get rid of all bitterness,
rage and anger, brawling and slander, along with every
form of malice. Be kind and compassionate to one another,
forgiving each other, just as in Christ God forgave you."
-Ephesians 4:30-32*

Forgiveness. I can feel some of the cringing that might have happened as you read that word. It's not a comfortable one, that's for sure. Forgiveness is hard! Maybe you've been hurt by someone you love, and forgiveness seems like the last thing you would ever want to do. Maybe it's you that needs the forgiveness from someone else. Or maybe you need to forgive yourself. Quite possibly, you've walked through a journey of forgiveness and have an amazing testimony about it. If that's the case, I would love to hear about it! Seriously, email me, Instagram me, write me a letter, just get in touch.

Since I know how hard it can be to open up about our experiences with forgiveness, I'll open the floor with something personal. I firmly believe that in our vulnerability we can connect and grow in powerful ways, and because of that I always want my life to be an open book. When I was very young, my dad was unfaithful and left my mom with my sister and me. We attempted the shared custody thing, but the only consistency was broken promises. I didn't see or hear from my dad the majority of my childhood. Meanwhile, we walked through a lot of other brokenness and destruction as a family.

In junior high I went away to winter camp, and for the first time I really let myself feel all that I had been carrying. I wrote a letter to God pouring out my heart, and I heard Him speak over me promises...promises that He would never abandon or forsake me. He also gave me an assurance that He is faithful in keeping those promises. The very things I lacked in an earthly father, He fulfilled as my Heavenly father. That's where my healing began. I wasn't ready yet to forgive, but God was softening and preparing my heart for it before I even knew that's where I was headed.

It took a lot of healing, working through emotions, and a few more broken promises before I was able to forgive my dad. And when I did, I saw him with new eyes. Something a mentor said to me in high school changed the way I thought about forgiveness. She said, "Tara, forgiveness isn't letting him off the hook and pretending like everything is ok. It's something between you and God." That advice right there has stuck with me. We can forgive and still be aware of the weight of what happened. Forgiving brings us freedom. I forgave my dad in my heart before I actually told him. The forgiveness that happened in private was deep and healing and peace-giving. It had more to do with me and God. The forgiveness I extended outwardly was a sense of closure of past hurt with my dad and a healthy boundary for the future.

If you are struggling with forgiveness, in whatever facet that might be, remember that it isn't about forgetting or letting someone "off the hook". It's a faith and a trust thing. It's a freedom thing. Let it go, sister. Just let it go.

Pray with me: *Lord, thank you first and foremost for your forgiveness in my life. I know I fall short often and you are so gracious to give me a clean slate every time. Teach me how to forgive like you do. Heal and soften my heart, adjust my perspective where need be, and help me to trust you in the process. Amen!*

Notes

Reluctance

"Have I not commanded you? Be strong and courageous.
Do not be afraid; do not be discouraged. For the Lord
your God will be with you wherever you go."
-Joshua 1:9

I ran into a friend at the store one day and somehow, we got onto the topic of how our reluctance in life is often related to fear. She shared with me her dream of doing real estate. I had never known that about her, but I could totally see her doing it successfully. I shared about my occasional reluctance with writing as I got closer to submitting my manuscript for this book. We went on about our business and it was a good reminder for me to just "keep going". Fast forward to later that night. As I was putting my daughter to bed, I told her I couldn't snuggle for the 57 demanded hours because I was going to do some writing. She responded with, "Your book is trash. You should just throw it in the trash, Mommy." I kid you not.

Her four-year-old insult hit me right in the gut. I know she didn't mean it. She is a kind-hearted girl and had no idea that her desperate attempt to get me to stay longer held any sort of power. But, I won't pretend it didn't hurt. As I left her room my eyes stung hot with tears. I had to ask myself why it bothered me so much. It didn't take long to figure it out. She spoke my fears out loud.

The closer I got to the end of writing my manuscript for this devotional, the more I felt reluctant to sit down and get more words out. This book you're reading is a project I've been extremely passionate and excited about for a while now. It is truly a dream come true, to be honest. But would anyone actually buy it? If they bought it, would they actually read it and would it actually have an impact? I had prayed big prayers that this book would encourage the hearts and minds of women all over. So, it makes sense that Satan was trying to keep me in a place of fear. No one grows or changes there. No one does great things out of fear.

I decided that to finish this thing I would need to, as Jessica Honegger talks about in her book *Imperfect Courage*, "go scared!" For me that meant that I needed to acknowledge that the fear was there causing that unrest in my soul about completing and submitting my work. It also meant that I needed to just do the very next thing and not try to think too far in advance. You know, actually practice what I preach and TRUST the one who gave me this venture in the first place. If I was sitting down for a cup of coffee with you, I would ask you what your dream is. Then I'd remind you that we are all scared and vulnerable, but we can't park there. We can't allow our fears to dictate our future.

Pray with me: Jesus, thank you for being a God who knows our deepest fears and also a God who is so much greater than them. Remind us of your great love and amazing plans for us when we feel scared and uncertain. Build a boldness and a courage in us that is not of ourselves, but of you. Help us to trust you as we take the next step in whatever season of life or opportunity you've called us into.

Notes

He did not
give us a
spirit of fear

GO BOLDLY!

Go Boldly

"For the Spirit God gave us does not make us timid,
but gives us power, love and self-discipline."
-2 Timothy 1:7

Do you have a dream? Something you've always wanted to do or be or accomplish? A big lofty goal you think you'll never be able to reach? I find it so sad to see people around me who are incredibly talented and hear that they never went for their dreams or currently aren't pursuing their dreams because they don't believe they are talented enough, or strong enough, or brave enough. It makes me sad, because it's easy for me to see the potential in others. Maybe that's why I love teaching so much. I get to see and grow the potential in so many little lives. It's always hardest to see the potential in yourself, though.

From the time I was a little girl I loved books. Even before I could read I was fascinated by them. I remember the first time I ever stepped into our county library with my Grammy. It was magical. A fascination with books grew into a love of writing—stories, poems, terribly cheesy song lyrics, etc. I remember gifting a Mother's Day poem to my mom in junior high. I can't remember what it said, but I do remember how it felt giving it to her—like it was the best gift I could possibly give her. I went on to love every English class I took.

Before realizing I wanted to be a teacher (and writer) I obtained my bachelor's degree in Business Administration. As a part of my program, I had to pass a writing exam. I figured it would be a breeze, and even after taking it I was confident I had aced it. A couple weeks later I received an email stating I had scored just two points under the required amount I needed to pass. Two points under? But, writing was my thing! I had expected to score above and beyond passing. It turns out they were looking for concise and direct writing, the kind of writing you would want in a business major (should have been a big fat hint for me). I ended up retaking it and writing what they were looking for. Even though I knew it was just a different style of writing they wanted, it really planted a seed of doubt in my mind as to whether or not I was any good at writing.

Fast forward seven years later to my teaching career. I was teaching my first graders how to brainstorm writing ideas and gave them the following prompt to practice with: "If I could do anything, it would be _____." I had them come up to the front one by one and write their dreams on the board. It was probably one of my most favorite days of my career thus far and something I will repeat with every class from now on. We got to the end and as I was transitioning into the next step, a student stopped me and asked what my dream was. Soon, the whole class was begging me to write my dream on the board. I stood there with a red Expo in my hand and questioned if I should even write it. Then I looked at their sweet little faces and decided that I should probably practice what I was preaching. I wrote: "Write a book". They squealed with excitement for me! At that moment, I knew I had to make this dream a reality.

If you are sitting there with a dream in your heart (no matter how big or small) and the idea of seeing it through gives you butterflies, then you probably need to listen. I believe God gives us dreams and desires that can bring Him great glory, if only we trust that He who made us is enough to accomplish those dreams in us. I may not ever become a famous author or have my work seen by thousands, but if it touches one woman's life then that is enough for me. This pursuit alone has already empowered me more than I could have ever imagined. Go boldly, ladies! Don't allow the doubts, fears or setbacks to determine how far you go.

Pray with me: *Lord, you are a God of big dreams! When I look at your creations all around me it encourages me and reminds me that so much is possible outside of me. Speak to my heart and develop those dreams and desires in me. Lead me in the way you would have me go to pursue these dreams. Quiet the fear and doubt that try to enter my mind and prevent me from moving forward. I give you all the glory and honor. Amen!*

Notes

Gratitude Trumps Attitude

"I will give thanks to the Lord because of his righteousness; I will sing the praises of the name of the Lord Most High." - Psalm 7:17

Some days I wake up in a funk. I couldn't tell you why, but I'm sure you can possibly relate. One way I have learned to battle "the funk" is by practicing gratitude. Dictionary.com describes gratitude as "the quality or feeling of being grateful or thankful". Webster dictionary adds, "a readiness to show appreciation for and to return kindness". You guys, that's biblical right there. Practicing a feeling of gratitude leads us to a "readiness" to show our appreciation by then acting in kindness. I love that the feeling of gratitude produces action. Well, it can if we allow it to.

If you think about it, it's pretty hard to stay funky when you have so much to be thankful for. When we are walking through valleys where the circumstances of life seem to be crushing in on us from all sides, we've got to dig deep to find that gratitude. It is there. Start with the most basic provisions. Shelter, food, family, etc. Pray through those basic needs, thanking God for them. Then move to the harder ones—maybe the very ones that are causing you strife. For example, we went through an extremely long process with the sale of our last home. It was seriously painful at times. I had to force myself to thank God in the midst of it so He could change my attitude.

It went something like this: "Ok, God, this is pretty awful. I want this house to sell so we can pay off our student loans and move into our new home. I know I have things to be thankful for, but it's hard to think of them now. Ok, thank you that we have a home currently. Thank you that we get to move closer to work and family. Thank you that you are providing us a way to get out of college debt. Thank you that you already know the plan that lies ahead for this and it is GOOD. Thank you that you even care to hear my worries and fears and pleas for help. Thank you even more that you want to take it from me, so I can have freedom mentally and spiritually. Use this mess for the good of others. And so on…" It always starts awkwardly and with a little resistance, and then before you know it you've got pages of thank you's and praises.

Whatever you are walking through, friend, He sees you. Big or small, He cares about it because He loves you and desires for you to walk through life victoriously. Stake claim over your funk today and crush it with gratitude. Not today, Satan. Not today.

Pray with me: *Lord, you know what I'm walking through right now. You know my propensity to get into a funk and stay there, not giving any acknowledgment to all the wonderful things I have to be thankful for. Frankly, it's just hard to notice those things in the moment. Change my eyes, Lord. Help me to see from your perspective. Help me to immediately recognize when I am in a funk and have a bad attitude, and let my response be to crush it with gratitude. I know you desire for me to walk through life victoriously and that's what I want too. Thank you for caring for me and loving me perfectly. Amen.*

Notes

Habits

"But you are a chosen people, a royal priesthood, a holy nation, God's special possession, that you may declare the praises of him who called you out of darkness into his wonderful light."
-1 Peter 2:9

"No, in all these things we are more than conquerors through him who loved us. For I am sure that neither death nor life, nor angels nor rulers, nor things present nor things to come, nor powers, 39 nor height nor depth, nor anything else in all creation, will be able to separate us from the love of God in Christ Jesus our Lord."- Romans 8:37-39 (ESV)

I'm a worrier. I'm indecisive. I'm an over analyzer. I'm forgetful. Why is it that we feel the need to wear our bad habits around like name tags? Yes, these things about us might be true in the current season we are in (or maybe we've always struggled with them), but it's not *who* we are. The longer we allow our bad habits to define us, the longer we will limit ourselves to those habits.

I do struggle with worry, but it's not something that I can't be free of. By spending time in the Word and in prayer, I can protect my mind against worry and practice healthy ways to deal with unexpected circumstances. I tend to have a difficult time making decisions, but I can get down to the bottom of what makes me feel so uncertain. The more I practice making decisions assertively (even if it doesn't feel natural at first), the easier it will get. For every bad habit I have, there is a way to improve it. For a long time I thought those things owned me, but they were just limits created within my own mind.

God didn't create a bunch of messy, lazy worriers and procrastinators. He created children of His own image, full of talents and skills and desires. He created resiliency and adaptability and redemption. He knew before we were born how we'd struggle, and He also knew how we'd overcome. The weaknesses of our human nature inevitably show up, but we decide how long they're present and how much space they take up. Also, we don't beat ourselves up over them. No one is truly motivated by being put down, so don't try to use that method on yourself. It might work in the beginning, but a sustainable change requires a desire to be different—a passionate and a positive "why".

In education we use a buzzword called "self-efficacy". Basically, it is a belief in your innate ability to achieve goals. With my students, my goal is to decrease their affective filter, which includes anything that makes achieving the goal seem more difficult (i.e. distraction, boredom, poor self-esteem, etc.). Decreasing that filter increases their self-efficacy, allowing them to feel more capable of achieving their goal. Once a student believes they can do it, they almost always do. We have to apply this to our own lives. It might sound "elementary" (no pun intended), but we need to remove the obstacles that make it hard to focus or make us feel less capable of meeting our goals.

We are more than our bad habits. Let's be careful not to identify ourselves so closely to these things from now on, and instead focus our energy on claiming our God-given identities. If you want to be more on time, create a goal to start using timers. If you want to stop being so messy, dedicate a day a week to cleaning one area of your home. None of it is beyond you. I'm putting my big girl pants on right alongside you today and taking back my name.

Pray with me: Lord, you know the areas where I struggle. I want these areas of my life to be different, but I have not been diligent in changing them. I know that these things won't just disappear, so help me to be intentional about changing them. Whether that means creating a plan or calling in some accountability, help me to follow through. I know that my identity is in you alone and these are just small ways I can honor you in my day to day life. Walk with me through this, Jesus. Amen.

Notes

you are God's favorite

JABO BALDWIN

God's Favorite

"For he chose us in him before the creation of the world to be holy and blameless in his sight. In love he predestined us for adoption to sonship through Jesus Christ, in accordance with his pleasure and will— to the praise of his glorious grace, which he has freely given us in the One he loves."
-Ephesians 1:4-6

*M*y mother in law is one of the liveliest people you'll ever meet. Her 5'2" frame is packed full of spunk, adventure, and crazy generosity. She's always smiling and has the best laugh. She doesn't take life too seriously, but at the same time she knows how to be there for people intentionally as they walk through deep waters. She was a preschool teacher for over 35 years before she stepped into the role of chaplain at a local Christian school, where I began my teaching career as a first-grade teacher. It was pretty neat getting to work on the same campus for a few years. Every Tuesday, I'd arrive at school to a note of encouragement on my door. She always ended it with "You're God's favorite!"

This sweet sentiment is something she spoke over my husband throughout his childhood. I've always thought it was the cutest thing. But beyond the cute factor, there's something special about reading that. *You are God's favorite.* Put your name in there and say it to yourself out loud. I don't care how old or esteemed you are, that should put a smile on your face. I think the reason I love it so much is because it represents that personal connection we are all invited into with our Maker. We are his favorite creation. We are special and irreplaceable and personal to Him. Own that, friend.

Write it down on a note card and put it somewhere you'll see it. Then when you begin to sense that you don't feel His presence in your life or question your purpose for one reason or another, read it over and over again until you believe it. YOU were made on purpose for a purpose and you're His favorite. Live like you believe that today!

Pray with me: *Lord, thank you for loving me in personal ways. I don't always feel like I'm special or worthy but remind me today Lord that I am your favorite. Help me to walk as if I believe that. Let all that I do align with the fact that I am special and loved and preferred by you.*

Notes

_____

_____

_____

_____

_____

_____

_____

_____

_____

_____

_____

_____

_____

_____

_____

Anxious for Nothing

"Come to me, all you who are weary and burdened, and I will give you rest. Take my yoke upon you and learn from me, for I am gentle and humble in heart, and you will find rest for your souls. For my yoke is easy and my burden is light." -Matthew 11:28-30

"Peace I leave with you; my peace I give you. I do not give to you as the world gives. Do not let your hearts be troubled and do not be afraid." -John 14:27

According to the ADAA (Anxiety and Depression Association of America), anxiety disorders are the most common mental illness in the U.S., affecting 40 million adults every year. Maybe as education about the issue has increased so has our awareness, but it seems the number of anxious people walking around on this earth continues to skyrocket. As a teacher of first graders, I'd like to say I don't see it in my classroom but that would be a lie. It breaks my heart when I see such young people struggling with anxiety.

As a disclaimer, I have to say I completely understand that there comes a point where anxiety and/or depression is beyond dealing with on our own and might require medical intervention. This devotion is not about that degree of anxiety. The focus here is how we can work to stop anxiety in its tracks in our everyday life. We feel anxious when we have a misplaced dependence. A misplaced dependence is when we depend on anything or anyone other than God. Most often, that dependence is placed on ourselves.

We practice this false sense of control as a means of coping with an out-of-our-control situation, becoming dependent upon ourselves to find a solution and hope. No wonder we feel so anxious in these moments. Our hope is standing on shifting sand. That wasn't how God planned it. When we choose to be anxious over allowing God to take control in a certain area of our lives we are acting out in sin.

His plan for us all along was peace. He sent His son so that we could have freedom from sin and condemnation and know true peace. His desire for us when we enter into something overwhelming or intimidating is that we would be still. He wants to handle it for us; we just have to allow Him to. So, let's take our dependence and place it on the only ground we know is sure.

Pray with me: *Jesus, Prince of Peace, allow me to depend on you in all circumstances. When I start to take matters into my own hands and practice false control, reveal it to me. Show me what a contrast that is to what you have to offer me. Let me remember that I can simply surrender and be able to rest in your perfect peace. Let your truth rule in my heart and mind. Amen.*

Notes

His Great Name

"And I will do whatever you ask in my name, so that
the Father may be glorified in the Son. You may ask
me for anything in my name, and I will do it."
John 14:13-14

I love how powerful and personal names are. One of the first and biggest decisions we make as a parent is what we name our child. They will be called that name for the rest of their lives. It's part of their identity. My daughter has to name each and every one of her stuffed animals. Using my students' names in class is a way for me to make them feel seen and known. These things prove to me that when something has a name it has significance.

My high school youth pastor once encouraged us to place our names in scripture wherever we see Jesus is speaking. Wow, that changed scripture for me. No longer was it a book written hundreds of years ago to people that I don't know. It was a personal letter to me, Tara. Though our name is of greatest importance, there is still one greater—Jesus. Have you ever wondered why we end a prayer with "In Jesus' name, Amen"? The passage above from John tells us that whatever we pray or ask for in Jesus' name, we are praying according to the will of God. Jesus is our connection to the Father. When we pray in His name, we pray with authority and with great expectation.

I know a lot of people who are afraid to pray out loud, out of fear of lacking eloquence. An eloquent prayer is not what Jesus is looking for. He is looking for a prayer with a pure motive and a surrendered trust in His name. If all we could get ourselves to mutter is "Jesus", that would be enough. For His name has the power to overcome darkness with light. In His name, we are overcomers. I love the lyrics to the song "Your Great Name" by Natalie Grant. If you've never heard it, or it's been awhile, I'll give you a minute while you look it up.

She talks about how the sound of His great name can dissolve all that we're experiencing, including any ways the enemy might try to come up against us.

The name of Jesus is as powerful today as it was hundreds of years ago. It holds authority and power and is worthy of our praise. Let's call on His great name together.

Pray with me: Lord Jesus, you are mighty and powerful. How amazing it is that with the mention of your name the earth quakes and darkness gives way to light. What's even more amazing is that we have personal access to you. Let us remember the power we have in speaking your name over our lives and over our prayers. In Jesus' name we pray, Amen.

Notes

It is in
Christ
that we find out
who we are
and
what we are
living for

Identity

"God created man in His own image, in the image of God He created him; male and female He created them." - Genesis 1:26

"See what great love the Father has lavished on us, that we should be called children of God! And that is what we are! The reason the world does not know us is that it did not know him."- 1 John 3:1

She looks like super mom juggling baseball schedules and tending to booboos and temper tantrums with loads of grace and patience. She is well put together, well liked and well spoken. Little does anyone know she struggles deeply with insecurity. Her? Yes, her. She doesn't dare let it be known, because who would like her if they knew she was such a mess inside? No one wants to see that, much less be friends with that.

Maybe you've known her. Maybe you've been her. I know I have... well maybe not the part about the patience of an angel while her kid is throwing a tantrum at Target, but we'll save that one for another day. As women (and I know plenty of men who would agree as well), insecurity is one of our biggest struggles as humans. It starts young and it runs deep. Its mission is to destroy us in the darkness. For some women it's subtle... an underlying tension within that is triggered by certain situations or people. For others it is straight up debilitating. Where in the world does this come from and why does it seem to affect every woman I know?

The answer is simple. We have lost, or in some cases have never known, ourselves. I'm not talking about the whole "go out and find yourself in the world" mumbo jumbo. I'm talking about our God-given identities. Sister, did you know that God wrote an identity over you? Did you know He loves you SO much so that He decided to create you in His very own image? That means He designed you perfectly (i.e. no mistakes here!) to be exactly who you are, in this time, in this place. He created you and stamped His approval and His holiness on you right at that moment. There is nothing we could ever do to earn it or remove it...it has already been done.

So why are we hiding helplessly in the dark with this, when Jesus is the light that can instantly blow insecurity out of the water? Why are we looking to those around us to tell us or show us that we're good enough? (And who wants to just be "good enough" anyway?) Why are we scrolling social media and comparing our lives to the lives of other women who were also created in the image of God and were called to be themselves? No one else decides who we are. God did that. What a relief! So now that that's out of the way, let's spend our time living our best lives... living out that precious and perfect call He wrote over us before our first breath. Like my girl (I like to pretend we're friends in real life) Lysa Terkeurst says, "There is an abundant need in this world for your exact brand of beautiful." Believe it, friends!

Repeat after me: No one else decides who I am. I was chosen and designed on purpose, for a purpose. I am enough, because He says I am and that is enough for me.

Pray with me: *God, this is hard. It's one thing to tell my mind, but it's another thing to truly take it to heart. Please help me to believe in the woman you made me, whole-heartedly. Please focus my mind on who I am in you, and not who the world thinks or says I am. Please help me to hear your voice above the lies of the enemy that try to tell me that I'm either too much or not enough. Set me straight when*

I'm being stubborn and slipping back into old thought patterns of self-pity or comparison. God, thank you for loving me perfectly and creating me in your image. I truly want to live out my God-given identity and accomplish your will for my life. In your Holy name, Amen.

Notes

Image Bearers

"God created Man in His own image, in the image of God He created him; male and female He created them." -Genesis 1:27

he book of Genesis teaches us that God created man in His own image. What an honor to be created in the image of God. It's hard to even wrap my mind around, and I rarely consider the image of God when I think of myself. We are image bearers and with that comes a level of responsibility. To be honest with you, this entry sat on my desktop for weeks with nothing more than a title and a couple quick notes. It's obviously not one I was excited to write, because anytime you call people to accountability or responsibility it's a little uncomfortable. Plus, who am I to be calling anyone to this? I have a hard-enough time with it in my own life.

But as God often does, He wouldn't let me forget about this one. I finally opened it back up, and as I wrote He gave me the words. You guys, I am nowhere near a golden example of how to be an image bearer. I just know that being an image bearer was weaved into our very being and it's something we can't ignore. So, what does it even mean? It means that God literally created us to reflect Himself—His character.

Here is the hard part. As image bearers, we have a responsibility. Quite opposite of what the world tells us, our lives are not our own. We are not here to merely seek our own happiness and indulge in things we love. Our purpose is to bring light and hope to a broken world. We are to be His love with skin on, caring for those around us and building one another up. That doesn't mean our lives are boring, uneventful or void of things we love. On the contrary, God has filled us up with desires and dreams and all sorts of abilities, and He wants us to enjoy and utilize those things—just not for selfish gain.

As image bearers, people around us should see evidence of Jesus in us without us ever telling them we are believers. Our reflections in the mirror show us in our exact current state. This serves as a wonderful reminder. As we take an honest look at ourselves, we should consider how we're doing with reflecting more of Him and less of us. Are we giving people around us a good example of the unconditional love He pours out on us? Are we forgiving and showing grace? Are we sacrificing some comfort to be there for others?

These questions are not meant to overwhelm or make us feel like we are not enough—quite the opposite. They are to remind us that we were made enough and every day we live is a gift. If we live with our eyes on Jesus and our hearts open to growing and loving, everything else (all those reflections of His character) will fall into place. You are beyond capable, friend. I am too. Let's hold each other to this honor of image bearing.

Pray with me: *Father, thank you for the honor of being your reflection. We definitely don't feel worthy of that. Teach us what it looks like to be an image of you in our day to day lives. Mold and shape our hearts and minds to align with your character. Instead of feeling overwhelmed, let us feel hopeful and powerful. Give us the right people in our lives to hold us accountable in this. We love you, Lord. In Jesus' name, Amen.*

Notes

In Awe

The ocean, driving into Yosemite Valley, a Montana sunset, the birth of my children. These are the things I jotted down as I asked myself this question: what inspires awe in me? Think about that question for a second and come up with a couple things you might write down...actually, write them down. Not to be bossy, but there's something about seeing the words on paper in your own handwriting that makes them extra special. I'm so glad I wrote mine down. If I hadn't, I may not have ever written this entry. The next question I asked myself was: does God's word provoke this same sort of awe in me?

My stomach sank as I gave an honest answer of "no". I wanted it to, but it just didn't. Maybe you can relate. That honest moment changed something for me. I knew I had to look into essentially what the Bible says about itself and why it should inspire awe in me. I researched a bunch of scripture and could fill the entire page with references for you, but the three above are the ones I came across that really stood out to me. First, the word of God is ALIVE and active. It is relevant in our lives today and not only that, but Hebrews says it judges our heart attitudes and mindset. That means that as we read His word, the ugly parts of our heart and mind are exposed. With humility we accept those convictions and we allow Him to transform those areas in our lives. This is powerful.

Second, Psalms says His commands are TRUE. If I'm going to be sold out to something I have to believe 100% that it is right and true. We can rely on God's word because it stands against all questions and doubts. In it He reveals to us His character and how Jesus navigated this fallen world. It is the truth we can hold up all other ideas, thoughts and theories against, and then watch as they either line up or fall off. I am always finding new connections to the people and situations in scripture, and I love that it gets personal like that. His Word and its truth remain forever. They'll always be relevant, and they'll always be true.

Last, God's word is helpful. Not only does it help us to navigate life, but it is also helpful for building up and encouraging one another. Second Timothy tells us it is useful for teaching, rebuking, correcting, and training. Left to our own devices and strung together sentiments, we can fail miserably at being what people around us need. God's Word is the only source that when it goes out it does not come back empty. It always, always, always either plants, waters, or revives a seed in someone's life. Second Timothy goes on to say that it equips us for every good work.

It sounds too simple, right? If I just spend some time in God's word, I'll be equipped to do great things in the lives of people around me? Yes, it's that simple. So, why aren't we doing it more often? Let's change that. Let's be Bible reading girls, not for a checklist or a facade, but because we truly desire for it to change our hearts and minds—to inspire an awe in us that is incomparable.

Pray with me: *Lord, it is my desire to be sincerely in awe of you and of your Word. Develop this in me. Open my heart and mind as I dig into your Word. Grant me discernment and wisdom as I interpret scripture. Show me how it applies to my life and how I can use it to build up the people in my life. Speak to me through your Word, Lord. I'm ready to listen. Amen.*

Notes

If Christ were only a cistern we might soon exhaust His fullness But who can drain a fountain

CHARLES H. SPURGEON

Inexhaustible

"But because of his great love for us, God, who is rich in mercy, made us alive with Christ even when we were dead in transgressions—it is by grace you have been saved."
-Ephesians 2:4-5

Do you ever feel like you might exhaust God? Like at some point He is going to look down and be like, "Ok, hot mess woman, I can't take any more of your neediness." Ok, that is completely false thinking, but my mind has honestly gone there before. On the contrary, He wants us to be needy. The Bible says that's what God is looking for. He created us to need Him and to lean into Him. So, we're getting something right, ladies! I love this quote I heard once at a women's retreat. "If Christ were only a cistern, we might soon exhaust His fullness, but who can drain a fountain?"

I love it because it reminds me that He is vastly greater than we will ever know or comprehend. He has no end and can never be used up. My life is but a grain of sand and that means that the predicament I'm facing is even smaller. Not only is He more than capable of tolerating our needs, but He genuinely cares for us and loves us unconditionally and actively. His love fulfills us in ways we didn't know were possible. His love is intimate and intentional. It pursues us and fights for us.

So, no, we cannot exhaust the perfect and never-ending love of God. Perspective and a focus on His greatness is how we crush those moments of defeat. I love the way Cory Asbury describes God's love in his song "Reckless Love of God". Find a quiet place and play it as you spend some time in prayer and reflect on His inexhaustible love for you.

Pray with me: *Thank you, Father, that your love is enough for us. It's more than enough. It's infinite and omniscient. We can never exhaust you. Though we are small and finite, you care deeply about what hurts us. Thank you for fighting for and pursuing us with your perfect reckless love. When we enter into seasons of doubt or distress, let us lean into your love and be held there. In Jesus' name, Amen.*

Notes

Insecurity Wears a Mask

"When pride comes, then comes disgrace,
but with humility comes wisdom."
-Proverbs 11:2

"For by the grace given me I say to every one of you: Do
not think of yourself more highly than you ought, but rather
think of yourself with sober judgment, in accordance with the
faith God has distributed to each of you." -Romans 12:3

*I*nsecurity wears a mask—sometimes it's pride, a false sense of confidence, an outgoing demeanor, or even humility. These masks can make it hard to spot insecurity right away, but eventually it reveals itself. It's not our job to point out or judge insecurity in others, but it can help us to understand them. More importantly, being aware of the mask(s) that insecurity wears, helps us to understand ourselves.

When I'm feeling insecure, I typically don't walk around telling everyone about it. For me it's this underlying gnawing feeling that I don't really recognize until I react in a way that is incongruent with my normal behavior and personality. I've gotten better at recognizing it though. Or maybe it's that I've started to listen more when God is pointing it out in me. Insecurity often encourages us to act like a total fruit loop, but it's even more insidious than that. Insecurity is a hyper focus on self. So, we're walking around feeling like victims, when in reality we are being completely self-centered. What a trap!

Tell me the last time you felt insecure and simultaneously were able to love on and serve someone well. It's impossible. We can't be insecure and humble at the same time. Either our focus is inward or it's outward. When we are inwardly focused, that's all we can see. When we are outwardly focused, that self-centeredness diminishes, and we are able to shift our attention to the needs of those around us.

Maybe insecurity consumes you and this is a ground-breaking revelation for you. Maybe you struggle with it in one area of your life and otherwise have it "under wraps". Either way, I strongly believe God calls us to more—more than the trap of self-centeredness. I believe if we were able to have an out of body experience and look down at ourselves from a 3,000 foot view, we might just laugh (or maybe cringe) at our own pettiness. This life is so much BIGGER than us! Let's stop allowing the self-sabotage so we can experience all that God has for us. Amen?

Pray with me: *Lord, you know my propensity to be consumed by insecurity. You know the places where I struggle with it most. I pray that you would help me to shift my energy from being self-consumed to being self-aware. Help me to recognize a potential insecurity, bring it to you, and leave it there. Help me to read your truth instead of playing the tape of my own thoughts. Grant me a healthy mindset so that I can stop living as a victim and start living out your perfect will for my life and the lives of others. In Jesus' name, Amen.*

Notes

Judgy Judy

"Judge not, that you be not judged. For with the judgment you pronounce you will be judged, and with the measure you use it will be measured to you. Why do you see the speck that is in your brother's eye, but do not notice the log in your own eye?" -Matthew 7:1-3

"You, then, why do you judge your brother or sister? Or why do you treat them with contempt? For we will all stand before God's judgment seat. It is written: 'As surely as I live, says the Lord, every knee will bow before me; every tongue will acknowledge God.' So then, each of us will give an account of ourselves to God." -Romans 14:10-12

I cringed a little as I heard the screams coming from the next aisle. I couldn't see the source yet, but I knew all too well what was happening. A little girl no more than three was having a meltdown of epic proportions, and although I couldn't see that mama, I could feel her tension from a mile away. We pulled parallel into different check lines and the screams continued. I could feel the stares like daggers and the hushed comments all around. It made me uncomfortable, and I wasn't even the one with the screaming kid (this time).

I went on about my business and was handing my debit card to the cashier when the lady behind me leaned forward and muttered to me, "Wow, that lady needs to control her kid. Mine never acted like that." I believe every hair on my body stood up at that moment. It was all I could do to fight down the indignant girl inside me —the one that wanted to take my hoops off and snap as I told her "Girl, are you kidding me? Were you sleeping as you raised your children?"

Don't worry, I said something slightly more graceful and there was no removal of earrings. I turned around and told her that being a mom is just hard and that sometimes (lots of times) kids cry when you don't want them to, and if it were her in that situation I would hope other people would have a little more grace. She just stood there staring back at me with wide eyes. Part of me wanted to crawl into a hole for saying anything out loud and the other part of me wanted to take a bow.

As I walked out, I gave that exhausted mama a knowing nod, and vowed to never judge another mom again. Yes, I had stood up for her that time, but I had judged many a mom in my mind before (especially pre-kids). When it comes down to it, judgement comes from a place of insecurity. When we judge, we are saying or portraying that we know better than someone else. We're putting ourselves in a position of superiority, and who are we to do that?

We are all hot messes in need of grace. We're all just trying to do our best. When we choose to pretend we are beyond reproach and step into judgment, we invite judgment in for ourselves. I love that this topic is in the Bible. Obviously, He knew we'd struggle with it. God is the only one with any right to judge, and in the end, we will be judged based on how we chose to live this life. Don't give judgement a place in your story.

Pray with me: *God, please forgive me for the times I judge others. Help me to be aware of it in the future so I can change my perspective and check my heart. Reveal to me whatever it is inside of me that desires to pass judgement on others. Change my heart and mind in this area. Instead of seeing others with a critical eye, help me to see them as you see them. Amen.*

Notes

Labels

"But you are a chosen people, a royal priesthood, a holy nation, God's special possession, that you may declare the praises of him who called you out of darkness into his wonderful light."
-1 Peter 2:9

"See what great love the Father has lavished on us, that we should be called children of God! And that is what we are! The reason the world does not know us is that it did not know him."
-1 John 3:1

abels. We all wear them. We wear them on our clothes, and we wear them on our hearts. They are the words or phrases that tell us who we are, who we aren't, or who we're supposed to be. Sometimes these labels are self-adhered after we experience tragedy or loss. Sometimes (often times) these labels are placed on us by people we know and love. Maybe you've been called "needy", "overly sensitive", "a little much", "dumb", or "naive". Maybe you have acted in ways that live up to those things or maybe not. In some cases, people intend to hurt us by limiting us and labeling us. In other cases, they have no idea the words they throw at us are cutting deep into who we are.

No matter how they end up stuck to us, we have a decision to make. We are not defined by labels unless we decide to be. We decide if what is spoken over us is true, and we decide if we are going to allow those things to define us. When people speak negative or hurtful things over us, they are speaking out of their own limitations. It is their perception that drives them to speak their opinion, not the truth. It is our responsibility to be familiar enough with the voice of God that when labels are hurled our way, we immediately recognize them as falsehoods.

The one and only label we *should* concern ourselves with is: Child of God. This label tells us we are His. He is the one whose opinion matters. He is the one who created us, and He is the one doing a great work in us as we become the women He created us to be. He is chiseling us one day at a time like a master sculptor chisels away at a piece of stone. He chips off anything that doesn't align with His good purpose for us and polishes all the magnificent features He fashioned in us so intentionally. When we believe this with our whole hearts, all the other labels fall off. Maybe you've been wearing your labels for so long, you didn't realize you were someone else apart from them. I'm here to tell you that you are SO much more than those things. You are here for a purpose and the labels you've been wearing and believing are doing you no justice. You were made for more than this.

Pray with me: God, you know the labels I have worn. You know who they came from and how long I've been owning them. If there is hurt there, heal it Lord. Help me to identify the hurt and to one day be able to forgive the people who have knowingly or unknowingly hurt me in this way. Protect me from falling into the trap of living as a victim. I know you call me far higher than that. I am not a victim, for that would just be another label. I am yours. You call me fearfully and wonderfully made in your image. Continue to chisel me, taking away every part that isn't true or good. I trust you to do a great work in me. In Jesus' holy name, Amen.

Notes

Lord
I AM
who You say
I AM

Let it Go

*"You will keep in perfect peace those whose minds
are steadfast, because they trust in you."*
-Isaiah 26:3

"*W*hat other people think about you is none of your business. (original author unknown)." You know when you see or hear something so good you have to say it or hear it a few times to fully soak in all the greatness? That's how I felt when I heard this quote for the first time. It was an aha moment I should have known all along. Besides the fact that I am a recovering people pleaser and this quote could be my anthem, the reason this hit home so much is because it touches the deeper issue of identity. I am not who people say or think I am.

If I could go back in time and teach younger Tara one thing, it would be to stand firm and confident in who God made her. I spent so much time worrying over what people might think or already did think or maybe in the future would think of me. What a prison! I had no idea how much energy I was wasting not just being myself unapologetically. I had no idea that I was stifling creativity and all the other great things God could have been doing in and through me had I not been so wrapped up in my thoughts and insecurities.

I believe my people pleasing came from two places: a place of insecurity and a place of genuinely caring about others. Once I experienced enough hurt, I began to not only worry about what people thought, but I also worried about the intentions behind people's actions. Trust me, deal with enough passive aggressive people and you start to question everyone's intentions. I had to come to a place of surrender in this, and if you're struggling with that then listen carefully to this next line. If someone wants to say or do something kind with ill intent, take them at face value. Take the kindness and leave the rest. You can't control them or their intentions. Let God do that. Carrying their intentions or trying to decipher them isn't healthy. We've got enough burdens of our own to keep us plenty busy.

Drop the perception game. The people who love and care for you well, know who you are. More importantly, God knows who you are and who you will become. When you allow your mind to be steadfast and focused on Jesus alone, you will know who you are. So, let it go, girl, and revel in the freedom that was always meant to be yours!

Pray with me: *Jesus, you are the only one whose opinion matters. Please make me believe that wholeheartedly. When someone wrongs me or has ill intentions, help me to react in maturity. Help me to be able to see the truth alone and drop the rest. Teach me the freedom that comes from letting go so that I might rest in your perfect peace. In Jesus' name, Amen.*

Notes

$\mathcal{L}osing$ It

*"And my God will supply every need of yours
according to his riches in glory in Christ Jesus."*
-Philippians 4:19

*"But He said to me, 'My grace is sufficient for you,
for my power is made perfect in weakness.' Therefore,
I will boast all the more gladly of my weaknesses, so
that the power of Christ may rest upon me."*
-2 Corinthians 12:9

As a youth pastor's wife, my summers are full of what I've come to call "single mom weeks". My husband's work is definitely kingdom work and I love that it's his job to bring young people to Christ. If I'm real honest though, in these weeks where I'm doing the solo- mom-of-little-people thing, I don't usually feel on my game. It's during these times where I'm more exhausted and spent than usual that I find myself losing it on my kids. The hardest part for me is getting a reign on my reactions.

I don't know about you, but some days I just feel like I can't get off the struggle bus. I strive to react in ways that are appropriate and effective and God honoring. Every once in a while, I have days where things are going smoothly, and I feel successful in this area. But, often I find myself in a pit of mom-guilt, very much in need of grace and forgiveness. There's good news though. I know I'm called to move past this place—the one where I get frustrated and yell at my kids, have a disrespectful tone with my husband, or panic when something happens that was outside of my plans or expectations.

I definitely don't have things all figured out here, but I have learned a couple of ways to combat and prevent reactions. When I take an honest look at what leads up to my reactions, I notice a common theme. I'm almost always preoccupied. This preoccupation, whether mentally or physically, is the precursor to me feeling like I can't "handle" what's in front of me at the moment.

Here's an example to put things into perspective. I'm standing in the kitchen scrolling my phone for recipes, so I can create our weekly menu, and in the background, I hear the noise level in the playroom start to rise (i.e. It's about to go down). I ignore it because, hello I'm busy here. Pretty soon I hear crying and I have kids running to me tattling. Because they completely interrupted my scroll and plan, I snap at them and am not in the right headspace to deal gracefully with the sister who has stolen the toy car from her baby brother for the fifteenth time or the brother who has hit said sister because said toy car was stolen.

Now, I'm not saying that we need to sit around doing nothing while we wait for something to arise so we can be ready to handle it well. That would be absurd. I'm just pointing out that in my life, when I am preoccupied with something that I intend to stay preoccupied by, I tend to react in ways I wouldn't normally react. If I would have put my phone down and decided to finish planning after I investigated the increasing tension in the playroom, I would have been completely available to handle the issue gracefully and effectively.

I have a close group of girlfriends who I do a Bible/book study with. Over the last couple of years, we have created a safe place where we can be completely honest with one another. Through that, honest trust has been built and we now have relationships of great accountability. We all know that when we get a text saying, "Mean mom came out tonight", we drop what we're doing and get on our knees in prayer for that girl. It is hard being a mom and trying to balance a personal and a professional life with a parenting life. We also know that it's not impossible. We cling to the fact that in Jesus, all things are possible. If we allow Him to, He will chisel away at all those old habits and tendencies and replace them with new ones. He will pour out His grace in heaps and give us exactly what we need to respond well. I have seen the change in myself and in my friends as we commit these things to prayer. Are we perfect? No. Will we continue to make mistakes in this area? Most likely. But we are looking for progress friends, not perfection.

Pray with me: *Father, you know how hard this parenting thing is. You know how much we want to be the perfect mom for our kids—the one who never gets overwhelmed or snappy. We make so many mistakes and sometimes feel that we'll never move past this struggle, but we know that isn't the truth. We know that in you all things are possible, and we will stand on that truth and in your strength to do the job you have set before us. You call us to make progress, and that is what we intend to do. Enable us with the patience and grace and humility we need to continue growing in this area. Help us to put down our distractions and preoccupations. Provide positive relationships for us to lean on when we need that human support and accountability. We love you Jesus. Amen.*

Notes

Morning Meetings

"Give me understanding, so that I may keep your law and obey it with all my heart. Direct me in the path of your commands, for there I find delight. Turn my heart toward your statutes and not toward selfish gain. Turn my eyes away from worthless things; preserve my life according to your word."- Psalm 119: 34-37

At some points in my life, reading my Bible and going to church have felt like checks on my spiritual to-do list rather than food for my soul. It's so easy to get into a habit of something and forget the real reason we do it in the first place. Religious ritual without heart is empty. Imagine how much more we would gain if we really were honest with ourselves about why we do the things we do. Is it out of obligation? Do we feel guilty if we don't? Are we doing it for others?

God designed the Bible and church to meet all of our needs as we live out the mission of loving others and bringing Him glory. If our religious practices are laced with obligation, reluctance or condemnation, then maybe it's time to go back to the basics. Maybe it's time to revisit the gospel and make ourselves see the reality of what Jesus did for us all over again. Has that been lost on us just because we have read or heard it so many times?

I have definitely been there, and not that long ago either. It makes me sad to think about all the years I missed out on what God could have been speaking to my heart if only I would have slowed down and listened. What word would He have given me for my day or for someone else? It doesn't help to live in regret, but I do think it's healthy to stop for a minute and be real with ourselves.

Since I have started the discipline of getting up each morning and giving my first moments to time with Him, my heart has changed. I'll be honest, it didn't feel very natural at first. I was tired and counting down the seconds to when the coffee would finish brewing. Then something changed. The more I showed up expecting to hear from Him and surrendering my worry and fear, the more I felt Him near me. He says in His word that He never leaves us. On the other hand, I think it's possible that we distance ourselves from Him.

I now crave those morning moments. I feel full and capable of offering something worthwhile to my family, my coworkers, my students, and others He places in my path. You can't pour from an empty cup, so make sure you're filling up before you go about your day. Blast some worship music, forget about any format or picture-perfect quiet time and ask the hard questions. Let's present ourselves before our Lord, asking Him to make our hearts and minds right. Then, let's be still. There's bound to be a heart change.

Pray with me: *Lord, thank you for wanting to spend time with me. Forgive me for the times in my life where I wrote it off as boring or something I didn't have the time for. I desire to know you intimately and to spend time with you daily. I desire for you to speak to my heart and fill my cup daily. Give me the energy I need to wake up and show up. Give me the endurance I need to keep showing up each day. Change my heart to love it. Amen.*

Notes

progress

OVER

perfection

Progress Over Perfection

"Not that I have already obtained all this, or have already arrived at my goal, but I press on to take hold of that for which Christ Jesus took hold of me. Brothers and sisters, I do not consider myself yet to have taken hold of it. But one thing I do: Forgetting what is behind and straining toward what is ahead, I press on toward the goal to win the prize for which God has called me heavenward in Christ Jesus." -Philippians 3:12-14 (ESV)

I don't know where you're at in your life or in your walk with God, but I'm sure you've got goals. For me, I'm constantly trying to grow and better myself, not because that's where my worth is, but because I love to learn. I know I'm called to greater things even when I don't feel like it. Maybe your goal is to run a marathon. Maybe it's to get in the Word daily. Maybe you want to pay off debt or be a more patient mom (me too). On the road to achieving our goals we are often held paralyzed by the trap of perfection.

What I mean by that is, we often don't have a whole lot of grace or grit when it comes to reaching our goals, or even making goals for that matter. We want the end result, without experiencing the journey. We want it to be easy. And when it isn't, when we fall short of perfection, we want to throw in the towel. "I want to be a more patient mom, but after all that praying and desiring for more in my motherhood journey, I just lost it on my kids like a fool. Forget it, I'll never be more than what I currently am in this area." Lies! Big fat lies! You know who is feeding us that inner dialogue? Satan. And you know who's eating it right up? We are.

We've spent so long tied to our ways and those things are not going to change overnight, try as we might. So, here's what we do. We surrender. We try in HIS power. Then, when we fall short (which we will), we give ourselves grace like our Heavenly Father does. But we don't stop there. Nope, we dust ourselves off and get right back at it. Not tomorrow, right in that moment. We're not going to let the lies of Satan keep us from becoming who God has called us to be. It's about progress, sister, not perfection!

Pray with me: Lord, I need to get it out of my head that I'm called to perfection. You are perfect, and you call me to be like you, but you do not call me to live tied to the weight of perfection. You know the desires of my heart and the ways I want to grow and meet goals. You planted those very things in me. I want to honor you with them and also with the journey in getting there. God, help me to give myself some grace when I fall short. Protect my mind from the lies of the enemy. When I start to hear that old familiar tape playing, give me the power to stop it in its tracks and cling to truth. Holy Spirit walk with me as I try in your power to be the best I can be...the me that you created me to be. Remind me that the goal is progress and not perfection. Amen!

Notes

Offended

*"Good sense makes one slow to anger, and it
is his glory to overlook an offense."*
- Proverbs 19:11

*"Know this, my beloved brothers: let every person
be quick to hear, slow to speak, slow to anger."*
- James 1:19

Sometimes people say careless things. I can't even count the number of times I've heard someone let loose a careless and hurtful comment with no reserve. I remember the comments toward the end of both my pregnancies. "Man, you're really about to pop! Are you sure there aren't two in there?" Yeah lady, I'm sure and you don't even want to know what else I'm sure of right about now. In those moments, how do we feel anything but offended? Is it even possible?

The truth is, when we feel offended we should check our heart. The way we react to an offense is usually more of an indicator for us than it is about the other person. The last thing we want to do when we feel offended is to look to our own heart and determine whether or not it aligns with truth. We want to see the ugly in the other person and shake our heads and write them off. Yes, the other person might just be a mean person, but there's usually something behind why the action or word made us feel the way it did. The more truth you fill your mind and heart with, the less you will feel like a victim in this world.

In our humanity, we are only capable of handling and making sense of so much. Our minds are limited and are constantly led astray by our fickle emotions and desires. But in our holiness (because Christ is in us), we are capable of so much more. It's not to say that we won't sometimes fall into the trap of offense, because we probably will at times. But, hopefully we will recognize and surrender and quickly move forward. That's the important part—to not stay there. In Christ it is completely possible to live an unoffended life. What freedom!

Pray with me: God you know how hard it is for me to overlook an offense. When it comes down to it, I want to be liked and thought well of. It really bothers me when people say or do something that feels like a threat. Help me to check my heart in those moments where I am tempted to feel offended. Help me to ask myself the hard questions. Why is it that this bothers me so much? Is it that I am insecure in this certain area? Am I too concerned with what people think of me? In those moments set my mind straight and give me your truth to meditate on so I can stand strong in the face of temptation. I surrender this to you and I ask you to change my tendencies the way only you can. Amen.

Notes

Open Door

"Above all, love each other deeply, because love covers over a multitude of sins. Offer hospitality to one another without grumbling. Each of you should use whatever gift you have received to serve others, as faithful stewards of God's grace in its various forms." -1 Peter 4:8-10

I have always wanted to be an open-door woman. I know a couple of open-door women. One in particular I've known many years. She was my Bible study leader in junior high. I can't even count the times she let us pile in her living room or in her pool, leaving trails of crumbs, flip flops, and ridiculous junior high humor. She never acted bothered or burdened by it. She's still that way all these years later. In everything she says and does, she invites people in. When she says, "Come on over anytime!", she actually means it. If someone were to show up at her door to seek counsel or just chat over coffee, she would stop what she was doing and welcome them right on in. Good grief, I admire that.

What makes one person more hospitable than the next? I do think in part that hospitality is a gift. But, I also think we (preaching to my own heart here) make too much of what hospitality should look like. We place too much clout on *how* to be hospitable the "right" way rather than *why* we should be hospitable in the first place. It's not about a perfectly clean home with a designer tablescape. Not that there's anything wrong with that. I love a great tablescape full of pretty things just as much as the next girl. Plus, I totally believe that talent can be used to invite people into the gospel in a very special way. But, that's not the goal for all of us. It's also not about an uninterrupted time in our schedule. It's not even about hosting well. It's about inviting people into our lives.

This is hard for me. I am self-proclaimed introverted extrovert. I get energy from being around people and crave relationship, but at the same time I need that time at home. I need that quiet space (well as quiet as it can be with two toddlers running amuck). I need that recharge. I have to be careful though, because that "recharge" time can become exclusive quickly. It's easy for me to get comfortable and shut the world out when I go home. For example, the last neighborhood we lived in we met two neighbors on our whole block in the three years we lived there. Isn't that bizarre to not know the people you live next to for years and years? There's something wrong with that when you think about it.

We have got to become more concerned with loving people than we are with having it all together and making things convenient. God has got a lot of work to do on me in this area. I think we can all start by evaluating our willingness to invite people in by asking ourselves a couple of simple questions. Am I willing to allow people to come into my life? Am I willing to sacrifice time, space and possibly resources to help people feel known and loved? What is one way I can be an "open-door woman" this week?

Pray with me: Lord, please help me to take an honest look at my openness to being hospitable. I know that you call us to love on and be there for one another using the gifts you have given us. It isn't always natural for me. Please show me practical ways I can do this. Soften my heart in this area and give me a God-sized perspective. Amen.

Notes

Overwhelm Me

"The Lord is my shepherd, I lack nothing. He makes me lie down in green pastures, he leads me beside quiet waters, he refreshes my soul. He guides me along the right paths for his name's sake."
- Psalm 23:1-3

I love this Psalm. It's such a thirst quencher for the soul. There was a time about two years ago where I felt completely overwhelmed. We had recently taken in a foster son and two months later I gave birth to my youngest. What a whirlwind! I remember feeling like I was juggling a million roles and tasks, always dropping something. I was in survival mode. When I am overwhelmed with this world or with the circumstances and responsibilities in my life, I want to wring out the words from these verses above and soak up every last drop. I think it's because there's such a desirable contrast between how I'm handling what I'm going through and what God wants for me to experience.

He calls us to rest. He calls us to allow Him, our good shepherd, to care for us and to take what we are carrying. The NLT version of this verse says, "The Lord is my shepherd, I have all that I need." When we feel overwhelmed, we typically either turn inward or outward for security and comfort. We want something to numb and to soothe our souls. For some people that means retreating and shutting out, for others it means stuffing down, and still others it means finding physical comfort in food or substances. But God calls us to look upward. He wants us to recognize that He is everything we could ever need. Do you believe that? Let me ask a different question. Do you live like you believe it? If the world saw you experiencing adversity, would they see you react in a way that reveals your upward glance— your trust in God's provision?

I know, that stings a little. Trust me, I'm preaching to my own heart here. Sister, I believe wholeheartedly that we were called to more, but not the kind of more that overwhelms us by all that we have yet to "do" or "be". He calls us to the kind of more that draws us deeper into trust and surrender. In actuality, this "more" requires "less"—less worry, less hustle, less numbing. He's calling us to more trust by letting go and resting with Him along those green pastures and quiet waters.

Pray with me: *Lord, thank you that you are the good shepherd who cares deeply for his sheep. When we feel overwhelmed you pour out your love and mercy on us and you desire for us to hand it over to you. Thank you that you want to take it from us and help me to remember that I have this "out". When I am overwhelmed, overwhelm me with your love. When I am tempted to turn inward or outward for comfort or reprieve, remind me to stop and look upward. Amen.*

Notes

Surrender
is a
prerequisite to
experiencing
His peace

Peace

"And let the peace of Christ rule in your hearts, to which indeed you were called in one body. And be thankful." -Colossians 3:15

"Peace I leave with you; my peace I give you. I do not give to you as the world gives. Do not let your hearts be troubled and do not be afraid." -John 14:27

"Peace: it does not mean to be in a place where there is no noise, trouble or hard work. It means to be in the midst of those things and still be calm in your heart." (Unknown)

The word peace is such a feel-good word. It has this passive, easy going vibe attached to it. Everyone wants it even if they cannot articulate what exactly "it" is. Bear with me while we dig into a little etymology for a second. The word peace occurs over 400 times in the Bible, so I figure it's important enough to know what it means right? The Hebrew word for peace is "shalom", meaning completeness, wholeness, fulfillment. I don't know which one of those words resonates most with you, but for me it is wholeness. When I lack peace in my heart and mind, I feel fearful and vulnerable. On the contrary when I have peace, I feel whole.

Let me clarify as to not minimize peace to a feeling, because it's SO much more than that. Peace is the result of our complete assurance in Christ to rule over our life. When we trust that He knows what He is doing and loves us enough to work out the details of our life in a way that benefits us and His kingdom, we can let go of our false sense of control and allow His perfect peace to settle into every corner of our soul. Peace gives us permission to take our hands off the wheel and then leave them off. This state of surrender is a prerequisite to experiencing His perfect peace. Like a drink of cool water to a parched soul, He refreshes and washes over all the dry and the weary places in us.

It was peace beyond understanding that carried me as I grew up without my dad. It was peace that assured my heart to step into a new career. It was peace that surrounded me as we walked through a tragic foster experience. It was peace that cradled me as I experienced a miscarriage. There's a reason you hear Jesus called the "Prince of Peace". He is the ultimate peace giver. There is no circumstance that is too big, too scary or too tragic for His peace to cover. His peace can be trusted, and I pray we can all receive it, because it is life changing.

Pray with me: *Lord, you are our Prince of Peace and we long to discover the perfect peace you have to offer. Your word says that you are the giver of peace and that when we accept that peace we are comforted, and we don't have to be afraid. When I am in the midst of chaos or uncertainty, remind me to reach out for your peace and truly accept it. It is your desire that we surrender the things that worry and burden us. Take these things, Jesus, and replace them with your perfect peace. We trust you. In Jesus' name, Amen.*

Notes

Sabbath

*"So, God blessed the seventh day and made it
holy because on it God rested from all his work
that he had done in creation." -Genesis 2:3*

*"There remains, then, a Sabbath-rest for the people of
God; for anyone who enters God's rest also rests from their
works, just as God did from his."-Hebrews 4:9-10 (NIV)*

abbath. I'm sure you've heard the word a time or two. Or maybe you're a Bible studying girl, and you know way more than I do on the matter. Either way, I'm trusting that you'll take something good away today, because the truth doesn't return empty, amen? I knew I wanted to write an entry on the sabbath, because I believe that anything that Jesus did regularly is worth paying attention to and imitating in our own lives. So, I studied up a bit on the history of the sabbath and also the ways we've gotten it wrong (we, meaning humanity in general).

We first see mention of the Sabbath in the creation story. Genesis 2 tells us that on the seventh day, He rested. Moving on into the book of Exodus, we see that Moses has to consistently remind the Israelites to observe the Sabbath and trust God to provide for their needs. Their biggest fear during this time was not having enough food to eat, and also the whole getting to the promised land bit. If I was in their shoes, trusting God to provide for every meal I ate, I may have struggled in the very same way. Moses reminds them to trust God for all provision by resting on the Sabbath.

Now if we jump on over to the New Testament we see the Pharisees have become pretty legalistic about the Sabbath. No longer is it about rest and right standing with God, but it is about rule following. In Mark 3:1-6 Jesus proves his point by healing a man's hand publicly in the synagogue on the Sabbath (making some major waves). Mark tells us that the Pharisees were completely appalled and that Jesus "grieved at their hardness of heart". Leave it to humans to change something holy and righteous and peaceful into something cold and heartless and meaningless.

So, is this call to keep the Sabbath holy still relevant in our lives today? Absolutely! God wants for His children to rest. But, it's not a passive rest. It doesn't mean spend one day a week devoted to Netflix binging and ice cream eating (although appealing) and let life happen. No, it means to come to Him with hands open, surrendering worry and fear and doubt. It means dropping in His lap all the ways you've strived to be good, accepted, and loved. It means modeling our rest after Jesus and the way He did the Sabbath, not by rules and obligations. May he reveal to you the ways He wants you to experience rest this week.

Pray with me: *Lord, thank you for teaching me in your word about the Sabbath. Thank you that you desire me to experience true rest. Thank you that you want me to feel free and at peace mentally, physically, and spiritually. Teach me what it looks like to take a Sabbath in my life. This week show me how to rest. Reveal to me the ways I strive in the wrong ways, seeking certainty about my identity and maybe even my salvation. Oh, how I long to experience rest. Show me how, Jesus. Amen.*

Notes

Self-Care

"Don't you know that you yourselves are God's temple and that God's Spirit dwells in your midst?" -1 Corinthians 3:16

$\mathcal{E}$ ver feel completely exhausted and in need of a break? (And every woman everywhere raised their hand and said "Amen!") As a full-time teacher, wife, mom, and writer my plate gets full, and some days I just need a break. A couple Saturdays ago I treated myself to a pedicure while my kids napped at home on my husband's watch. As I was sitting in the massage chair trying to figure out how to get it off "flap" mode (Is there anyone in the world who enjoys that setting?) my mind wandered back to my kids. What if they woke up while I was still gone? I would be missing time with them and also not getting done a plethora of things that needed to be done around the house that weekend. I'm proud to say I stopped that mom guilt in its tracks and enjoyed the rest of my pedi, but, goodness, can a girl catch a break?

Why does self-care seem like such a selfish thing? I wanted to know what the Bible had to say about it. 1 Corinthians 3:16 says that our bodies are the temples in which the Holy Spirit resides. Hebrews 4 talks about how we are to rest as God did when he created the world. What an amazing reminder for us to read that taking care of our bodies is Biblical. I cannot give all that I need to give and be all that I need to be physically and mentally if I am not taking care of myself. The Bible tells us that Satan is prowling around like a lion ready to devour and destroy. He is cunning in his ways, so it makes sense that he would warp the way we view self-care. He doesn't want us to be well rested and mentally refreshed so that we can continue to do great things. Of course, he would tap into our mama hearts and twist the truth, leading us to believe that denying ourselves a healthy lifestyle is being "dedicated" and "sacrificial".

The good news is that God knew long before now that women would struggle in this area. He knows our hearts and our desires. He also knows our physical and mental limitations and the things that can refresh us. I know one hundred percent that when I take those moments for myself to relax or to do something enjoyable, I feel more capable of handling the things God has given me. Take a moment today and consider how you are caring for yourself. If you are someone who struggles with feeling guilty when you take a moment for yourself, pray through that and ask God to show you the truth. He is for us, friends!

Pray with me: *Lord, you are the giver of all good things. You want us to find rest and to be refreshed so that we can carry out your good will. Show us healthy ways that we can put self-care into practice in our lives. Then when we go do those things, protect our minds from the attacks of the enemy. Let the guilt fall off and allow us to see only your truth. Thank you that you are for us, Jesus. In your holy name, Amen.*

Notes

Stinky Trash Can

"Do everything without grumbling or arguing, so that you may become blameless and pure, children of God without fault in a warped and crooked generation. Then you will shine among them like stars in the sky as you hold firmly to the word of life. And then I will be able to boast on the day of Christ that I did not run or labor in vain." - Philippians 2:14-16

I have a confession to make. . .I'm a recovering complainer. Ugh, I don't even like to claim that part of me, but without shining light on the dark and ugly places within us then how will those things ever change? I've come a LONG way, but I'm still a work in progress. I can't stand to be around people who complain all the time, so I never understand why I think it's ok if I do it (even if only in my mind). I am an elementary teacher, and at the start of every year I use "the trash can analogy" in hopes of squashing any attitude issues. Basically, a bad attitude is like a stinky trash can. It only takes one piece of trash (or one bad attitude) to smell up an entire room. Yes, the analogy might be a little elementary, but it's pretty profound, am I right? When we have an awful attitude, it affects everyone around us.

So why do we get into these ruts of bad attitudes and complaining? The answer really is simple. We get into these ruts because our eyes are focused inward. We unknowingly perceive the world around us through lenses that show us at the center of the universe. We're irritated by things happening to us, we're offended by people and situations, we're. . . acting completely selfish. Sorry if that hit a little hard, but usually the truth we need to hear doesn't feel comfortable.

If the problem is that our focus is inward, then our solution is to focus outward. When we take our eyes off of ourselves and start looking to the needs of others, complaining will fall off naturally. Take this example. Scenario one: A woman walks into a doctor's office. As she takes a seat in the waiting room, her head is full. She's irritated that there was traffic on the way there, annoyed that the room is full, wondering how long she will have to wait, offended that the gal at the front desk gave her a "rude" look, and so on. She sits as far as she can from anyone who might try to converse with her and she gets on her phone to pass the time.

Now for scenario two. A woman walks into a doctor's office. As she takes a seat in the waiting room, she notices the girl at the front desk seems stressed. She recognizes the look, because she's been there at least a zillion times herself and decides to break the ice with a smile and a compliment. She takes her seat next to another woman who is reading a book she has read before. She strikes up a conversation with the woman and they end up connecting on so many levels. Who knows where the unlikely friendship goes.

Same situation, different attitudes and outlooks. The point is, who knows what opportunities we miss when our focus is all about us—opportunities to be the light in someone's life, to encourage, to learn something, to GROW. I don't even want to think about the countless opportunities I've wasted. Let's be determined to look out and see the world around us the way God does.

Pray with me: Lord, you know my tendency to make things about me. I don't want to live selfishly. Reveal it to me right there in the moment when I am focusing inward rather than outward. Redirect my gaze to see things around me the way you do. Holy Spirit give me a nudge to say and do things for the people around me that will build up and bring life. Help me to do everything as if I was doing it for you...because really, I am. In your sweet and Holy name, Amen.

Notes

The B-i-b-l-e

"For the word of God is alive and active. Sharper than any double-edged sword, it penetrates even to dividing soul and spirit, joints and marrow; it judges the thoughts and attitudes of the heart." -Hebrews 4:12

"As the rain and the snow come down from heaven and do not return to it without watering the earth and making it bud and flourish, so that it yields seed for the sower and bread for the eater, so is my word that goes out from my mouth: It will not return to me empty, but will accomplish what I desire and achieve the purpose for which I sent it." -Isaiah 55:10-11

Raise your hand if you have a difficult time reading the Bible for yourself. Ok, I know I can't see you, but I would guess at least half of the women reading this book would throw a hand up for that. I definitely would have for the longest time. It's intimidating, foreign in some respects, and where do we even start? Maybe you haven't been intimidated by approaching the Bible and you've read it for years but struggle to connect with it. Either way ladies, we're missing out big time when we don't try.

Hebrews tells us that the Bible is alive and active and able to judge the heart and mind. It isn't some old book that we're supposed to read out of obligation. It is literally God's words written for us to teach us about His character and His love and His purpose for humanity. So, it's kind of a big deal. Isaiah goes on to say that just as the rain comes down from heaven and doesn't return, so His word does not return void. The messages of truth in the Bible get stored in our hearts and minds when we take the time to read and truly hear them.

I know from experience that when I commit to reading and soaking in the word of God, it transforms me. When I start my day off like that, I'm a little less "hot-mess Tara" and a whole lot more grace-filled—positive and confident in my identity. It's not a magic formula where you read and then gain super powers (although some days I have felt like that). It's intentional connecting with the word of God with the intent to grow and be changed for His glory. If you approach the Bible with an open heart and a prayer for God to reveal to you the truth of His word in a way that makes sense to you, He will most certainly provide. I'm excited for you to experience His Word in a whole new way. Set a quantifiable goal for yourself this week, even if it's small, and just see what happens.

Pray with me: Lord, I long to connect with the Bible. I know it's important in knowing you more and growing in my relationship with you. As I approach this holy book, grant me understanding and wisdom to interpret. Connect me with the right people and supporting resources to encourage me and keep me going. You tell us in your word that you are with us always, so Jesus be with me in this too. Amen.

Notes

these
are the
good ol' days

The Good Ol' Days

*"Teach us to number our days, that we
may gain a heart of wisdom."*
-Psalm 90:12

*"Why, you do not even know what will happen
tomorrow. What is your life? You are a mist that
appears for a little while and then vanishes."*
-James 4:14

I was baking cookies the other day and as I looked up out the kitchen window, the site before me stopped me in my tracks. My husband had hooked up the hose to a plastic sprinkler head and he and two undie clad kiddos were running and squealing with delight. I wanted to freeze time right there and just keep on staring. It was such a simple and seemingly insignificant moment, but I got this heavy feeling inside as I watched them. It was equal parts heartbreaking and awakening. These are the good ol' days, I thought to myself. These are the memories we'll wish we could rewind time to live over again.

I don't want to miss it! How many of these good ol' days moments have already passed me by because I was preoccupied with work or with scrolling on my phone or with being worried about something that didn't really matter in the grand scheme of things? Do you struggle with this at all—with being present? It's such a catch twenty-two. We want to be and do all things, and so we try hard and we run the rat race, but a lot of times we're totally missing it. Sometimes we're focusing on the wrong things. Or, maybe it's not even a focus on the wrong things, but just not enough focus on the right things. Life is happening, and time is passing whether we want it to or not.

Let's not waste any more time being preoccupied or stuck. Let's live life to the fullest. Read the book, take the vacation, bake the soufflé, put away the phone, and play in the sprinklers. As morbid as it sounds, we only have so much time left, and we just don't want to waste it. According to these verses, God doesn't want us to miss it either. He knew we would be prone to distraction and wandering. He knew how hard it would be for us to just be still and enjoy.

Pray with me: *Lord, you know our propensity to try and live ahead of the moment and be distracted by the demands and desires of the world. You know how shallow and short lived that is for our souls and you long to give us more of the deep, the meaningful and the simple. Forgive us, Lord, for when we miss the mark. Remind us that you created us to be full and bold and deep. Help us to be present in our relationships and to relish in the good ol' days while we're still living them. Amen.*

Notes

The Three Letter Word

*"A best yes is you playing your part in God's plan.
If you know it and believe it, you'll live it."*
-Lysa Terkeurst

*"I used to think you had to be special for God to use you.
Now I know you simply need to say yes." -Bob Goff*

Yes. A word made up of only three letters, but with so much power. The answer to some of the most life changing moments yet also the answer that can lead to exhaustion and depletion. If you haven't read Lysa Terkeurst's book, "The Best Yes," do yourself a favor and just hop on Amazon right now. It is so full of practical ways to give your best yes in life. After reading this book I took a good hard look at what I was saying yes to in my life, and also what I hadn't said yes to enough. It was far more revealing than I expected.

How many of you are people pleasers out there? Yep, I hear ya. In some ways, this can be a strength because we possess a certain level of compassion and consideration for those around us that is refreshing and God honoring. However, it can also be a curse. When we start to allow what others think of us to determine how we think and act, it's a problem— especially when we care more about what people think than what God thinks.

Some people want to say yes because they don't want people to think they aren't dependable or capable or thoughtful. Some people just like to be busy to keep their mind off of what's hard in their life. Ask yourself right now if there are any areas of your life where you might be saying "yes" for the wrong reasons. Furthermore, ask yourself if there might be places where you are saying "yes", when you should be saying "no"—not because it's a bad thing but because it is replacing time and energy you should be spending elsewhere.

Are our current yeses taking the place of what God's yeses are for us? I think so often we live with the short term in mind rather than the big picture. Are we just letting life happen *to* us? What if God's plans for us are WAY bigger (spoiler alert, they ARE) than what we are currently allowing in our lives? What if saying yes in the small but right ways led to big God honoring actions?

We are all in different seasons of life. For some, maybe saying yes to more intentional time with our family rather than 10 million weekly commitments is the change we need to make. For others maybe, it's saying no to phone scrolling or T.V. so we can put in the time on that book God has been calling us to write (eh hem, that was me!). Whatever it is that is keeping you from giving your best yes in the best places, get honest with yourself and bring it before the Lord. He knows where He wants your yes to be yes and your no to be no. He is ready to use you in big ways, so start living as if you believe that. . .then eventually you will!

Pray with me: *God, I know you are capable of doing immeasurably more than I can imagine—even with and in me. I pray you would reveal to me where I'm giving too much time and energy, and also where maybe I'm not giving enough. Make the motives behind my yeses be clear and let the only approval I seek be yours. I'm ready for you to do big things in and through me. Amen.*

Notes

Rock What You Got

"So, we, though many, are one body in Christ, and individually members one of another. Having gifts that differ according to the grace given to us, let us use them: if prophecy, in proportion to our faith; if service, in our serving; the one who teaches, in his teaching; the one who exhorts, in his exhortation; the one who contributes, in generosity; the one who leads, with zeal; the one who does acts of mercy, with cheerfulness."
- Romans 12:5-8 (ESV)

I love how this passage in Romans talks about us being of one body in Christ, each of us contributing and working together for the good of the body. It goes on to say the gifts we are given differ according to the grace given to us. Have you ever considered what your gift(s) might be? Have you ever felt like it's easier to see the gifts in others than it is to see the gifts in yourself? Me too, girl.

For the longest time, I considered myself mediocre when it came to talent or giftedness. I just felt like I never really had one thing that I was exceptionally good at. I mean I was somewhat good at things here and there, but nothing really stood out for me. I figured I must have missed out on the whole spiritual gift thing. The truth was, I didn't recognize the gifts I had as gifts.

As we read in the passage above, our gifts are going to be different. They're going to be just what God planned for us in this time period, in this place, in this season. So, comparing the giftedness of others to our own giftedness isn't an effective use of our time. When you receive a gift, you have to unwrap it in order to use it. If I'm gifted at singing (which I'm definitely not, but if I was) and I never use my voice for the Lord, then I'm not truly tapping into that gift the way it was intended. I cannot be fully blessed by it nor bless others with it, if I'm not honoring God with it. Another factor that is at play here is the unwillingness to claim a gift. I think some of us are so afraid of sounding prideful if we admit to being good at something. Or maybe it's that we're afraid of admitting we have gift-based dreams. I have struggled here as well. The truth is, we rob the world of what God could do through us when we deny the great things God is doing in us.

So here it is. My gifts are: encouragement (more specifically written encouragement), creativity, and teaching. For the longest time, I never considered these to be gifts. God has shown me how I can use these gifts in the lives of those around me, and never am I more blessed than when I'm using what God gave me for His people. Sometimes I will be sitting there in prayer or doing a devotional in the morning and I just feel God nudging me to text someone a little encouragement. It never fails that it's exactly what they needed to hear that day. He knows. Even when we don't, He knows.

That's why it's so important to say yes with our gifts. We can literally walk out the will of God when each of us is working together with our gifts. That's powerful! I'm sure I've missed out on tons of opportunities to use my gifts, but I'm shifting my focus forward to use them as much as possible from here on out. Are you with me? What are your gifts? Think on that today. Journal it. Then talk to someone you trust about it. I guarantee they already saw those things in you.

Pray with me: *Lord, you know my propensity to discount my areas of giftedness. Please reveal to me the gifts you have so graciously given me, so that I can use them for your will. It excites me to think about what you will do through me and it feels good that you have written these unique gifts over me as a part of my identity. Lead me in rich conversation over these areas. Stir in me ways you'd like me to say yes, even if it's just sending a simple text message. Make me brave with my gifts! You are the giver of all good things. Amen!*

Notes

instead of
circling it in
worry and fear,
circle it in
prayer

The Wait

"Because of the Lord's great love, we are not consumed, for his compassions never fail. They are new every morning; great is your faithfulness." -Lamentations 3:22-23

"Let us hold fast to the confession of our hope without wavering, for he who promised is faithful." - Hebrews 10:23 (ESV)

Fifty-nine days is how long we waited prayerfully for God to bring us a buyer for our home. We got an offer and we were elated. Then, the very next day the offer was withdrawn. Twenty-five more days passed before we got the next offer, the one that sealed the deal. So, for eighty-four days we waited and prayed faithfully for our buyer to come. For 84 days we sat there in the wait...in the uncomfortable. The "get me out of this already". The "isn't it time for the next step, God?" That wait. I'm just gonna go ahead and say it...waiting stinks with a capital S.

However, I had seen God provide and work for the good in my life and others' lives way too many times to stop trusting Him at this point. Yes, at times I felt irritated that we didn't know the timeline (hello, planner here!) and frustrated that someone hadn't bought our house yet because it really was a beautiful home we had grown to love.I didn't park there in those thoughts for long though. I couldn't, because I know myself too well (cue the crazy anxious thoughts). There's no way I was going to give into doubt and fear. I had to completely trust whatever it was that God had in mind, even if it wasn't what we thought.

Trusting in God isn't a magical switch though. After that initial surrender, I had to keep giving it back to Him again and again on a daily basis. With every showing that didn't turn into an offer and every piece of feedback that wasn't what we wanted to hear, I was tempted to take it back into my grip of false control. I had to daily put my hands out and give it to Him. Instead of circling it in worry and fear, I circled it in prayer.

If you are in a waiting seasons like we were, hang in there. I know how hard it is friend, but don't give up hope because things aren't going according to your timeline. Maybe what God has in store is way bigger and better than what you thought you wanted or when you thought you wanted it. Consider what He wants to teach you in this wait. He is good always —not just sometimes and not just for some people. Commit to prayer what you are waiting on and watch your attitude and perspective change big time. Sometimes it takes 84 days before you see Him answer, but trust in Him because He is faithful!

Pray with me: Lord, it is so hard to wait! It's uncomfortable and it usually requires me to stretch out of my comfort zone to let go of something I feel responsible for. Bring it to my attention when I am holding onto a false sense of control instead of trusting you. Forgive me for my lack of trust. I know you are the only one who is truly in control. Great is your faithfulness, Lord! Help me to live each day like I believe it. Amen!

Notes

The Words We Say

*"Do not let any unwholesome talk come out of your mouths,
but only what is helpful for building others up according
to their needs, that it may benefit those who listen."
-Ephesians 4:29*

*"May the words of my mouth and the meditation
of my heart be pleasing in your sight, Lord, my
Rock and my Redeemer." - Psalm 19:14*

If you've never read *The Five Love Languages* by Gary Chapman, do yourself a favor and read it. Then if you're a nerd like me and love to take quizzes to learn more about yourself, you should take the quiz and find out what your love languages are. One of my top love languages is words of affirmation. That came as no surprise to me. I have always given and received love through words of affirmation and encouragement. On the contrary, words can also cause great pain for me. Words hold weight and they reveal what the heart is storing up.

Because I'm a words person, I not only express love with my words but I consequently express anger and frustration with them as well. The place I find it hardest to use my words "for good" is in my home. Maybe it's that I feel most comfortable there to let all of me show. Maybe it's because I'm around my family the most and I see all of their flaws as well. I don't know what it is exactly, but I do know I want it to be different. I share this to tell you that I'm preachin' to my own heart here when I say that we need to watch our words. The tongue has the power to either build up or destroy.

I don't know how many discussions I've been in with my husband where a change in tone or a different entrance line would have ended the disagreement before it even started. We let words fly from our mouths without giving any consideration to the effects. Do we want to be right and heard more than we want to improve our relationships? Yikes. How scary it is to think that Satan could use us in his schemes to tear apart relationships and destroy self-esteems.

May the words we say reveal more of what we really mean. Let us send out powerful and uplifting words rather than discouragement and criticism.

Pray with me: *Lord, please tame my tongue. You know my tendency to lash out with my words, especially at home. Please make me aware of it when my heart is about to spew out ugly on my husband or my kids. Help me in the preventative work of storing up good in my heart and mind so that when I come to those moments I will be better equipped to hold my tongue or say something that is helpful rather than hurtful. Thank you that I don't have to try to change in my own strength. May the meditation of my heart and the words of my mouth be pleasing to you. Amen.*

Notes

Thought-life

"For though we live in the world, we do not wage war as the world does. The weapons we fight with are not the weapons of the world. On the contrary, they have divine power to demolish strongholds. We demolish arguments and every pretension that sets itself up against the knowledge of God, and we take captive every thought to make it obedient to Christ."
- 2 Corinthians 10:3-5

For our honeymoon, my husband and I took a trip to Maui. We left less than 24 hours after the wedding and were over the moon about spending our days relaxing on the beaches of Hawaii. So, there we were, driving hand in hand in our rented convertible into Lahaina for dinner on the water. (Uh take me back, please!) We were almost there when I noticed a very in-shape and well-endowed woman jogging in her swimsuit (still not sure how that's a good idea, but that's beside the point) along the side of the road. Immediately, I let my thoughts run wild and misjudged a look out his window to mean my husband was most likely noticing her and consequently measuring up my small chest to hers. Ridiculous, am I right? What's worse is, I stewed on it so much the rest of the drive that by the time we got to dinner I was acting mad at him. Poor guy didn't have a clue.

Thank the Lord I have matured a bit since then. I can guess maybe you've been through a time or two where you've let your thoughts run away with you and ended up somewhere you didn't want to be. We don't have control over that first thought that pops into our minds, but we do have a choice in how long we park there. If we do not take captive our thoughts, we are inviting them in.

As a pastor's wife and mom and teacher I have to regularly fight off thoughts about my worth and about my ability to do everything I need to do well. My mind hears things like: "You're dropping the ball, you're totally messing your kids up, you're not involved enough at the church, and you're not doing enough for your students." How dangerous that thought reel can be. What a slippery slope it is to listen to even one lie about ourselves.

In these instances, we have to ask ourselves a question: "Is this thought from God?" We can evaluate pretty quickly if it is or not. If the thought is not good or helpful, then it doesn't line up with what scripture says about the character of God and therefore it can't be true. Once we've realized it is not from God, then the choice comes in. We can either listen to that thought and see where it takes us (trust me it's never a positive thing), or we can choose to use the God-given authority within us to take the thought captive. Once that thought is taken captive it has no power over us. You guys, this is HUGE! We are not helpless in the battlefield of our minds. In fact, we've got some serious ammo to defeat the enemy's attempts to sabotage our thought life.

Pray with me: *Lord, thank you for giving me all the power I need to take captive unwanted thoughts. Help me to know your voice so that I can discern when I am hearing from you and when the enemy is trying to speak lies. Thank you that you care for me down to every thought that enters my mind. Amen.*

Notes

surrender
is a
sacred
act of
worship

When It Is More Than We Can Handle

"For we do not have a high priest who is unable to empathize with our weaknesses, but we have one who has been tempted in every way, just as we are-yet he did not sin."
-Hebrews 4:15

"Don't worry, God won't give you anything you can't handle." I've heard this phrase a plethora of times in an attempt to make someone feel better in times of sorrow or struggle. Naively I have doled out this phrase a time or two myself. I know the intention behind offering this phrase is pure and helpful, but the message itself is actually false. We have to be careful using Christian clichés like this that don't align with what God actually says in His word.

The truth is, God does give us more than we can handle, because He never intended for us to handle it on our own. He is the strength we tap into during those trying times. He is our rest and our peace in times of chaos and confusion. He is our provider when life's circumstances seem hopeless. It's all Him. And thank the Lord we don't have to "handle it" on our own, amen?

So, when you are experiencing a trial, call on the One who promises to carry it for you. Remind yourself it's ok to let go. It's more than ok—it's what He's calling us to do. Surrender is a sacred act of worship, even when we don't feel like what we're handing over is worshipful at all. When we open our hands up and let Him take whatever it is we're clinging to, we are exercising trust and humility. These things are God honoring. In our weakest moments we are actually strong. He is our strength and there is nothing that is more delightful to Him.

Pray with me: *Jesus, you are my strength in times of struggle and in times of joy. Please remind me to let my first response to adversity be surrender. When life feels like it's more than I can handle, remind me that all I have to do is be still and you will do the rest. It sometimes seems too simple an answer, but I know that you call me to this response for a reason. You know what is best for me at all times in all seasons. I trust you, Lord. Amen.*

Notes

Who Is He?

"Yes, my soul, find rest in God; my hope comes from him. Truly he is my rock and my salvation; he is my fortress, I will not be shaken. My salvation and my honor depend on God; he is my mighty rock, my refuge. Trust in him at all times, you people; pour out your hearts to him, for God is our refuge." -Psalm 62:5-8

I remember being asked this question at a Bible study in college once: "Who is God to you?" At this point I had been a believer for many years. This seemed like such a simple question, and yet somehow, I found it difficult to answer. I knew who He was, but I had never packaged it up and presented it out loud before. I listened as other people gave their answers and though there were some overlapping adjectives, each person unknowingly revealed a little snippet of their history as they explained who God was to them.

We typically come to know God in one of two ways: by what we are told or by how we experience Him personally. Sometimes, it's a combination of both. For some, God is a distant judge sitting aloof in the clouds waiting to cast judgment. For others God is like a close friend. For me He is my Father, my Redeemer, my Provider, my Peace and my Joy. The verses I share above from Psalm 62 are the ones I came across as I made the personal decision to follow Christ as a junior higher at winter camp. Reading about these attributes of God was a pivotal moment for me. It's hard to describe how it felt. I felt a peace wash over me—a settled assurance that I was loved, safe, held, and never forgotten.

The way we view God affects our trust in His ability to care for, love and provide for us. Those friends who viewed God as a distant judge consistently struggled to invite Him into personal situations where they needed His guidance or provision. Their view of Him was distant and impersonal, and consequently so was their faith in Him. Maybe you grew up with an unhealthy view of who God is. Maybe that was due to people in your life who were poor representations of what a believer looks and acts like. It is great to reflect and come to a realization about what could have distorted your view of God, but don't stay there. We have to be careful not to project the shortcomings of imperfect people on a perfect God.

Who is God to you? Take a few minutes today and reflect on that, even if you have done it a dozen times before. I find that we often recognize and appreciate different characteristics of His character as we walk through different stages of life. Forget about the church answers and be real with yourself. See if there are any discrepancies in the role He currently plays in your life versus what the Bible says about God's character. Knowing Him intimately changes everything about our faith.

Pray with me: *Lord, help me to know you more intimately. Show me the truth about your character and your provision so that I can trust you more. I want to know you and to be known by you. Help my mind and heart to agree with the truth of scripture and let any false perceptions fall off for good. In Jesus' name, Amen.*

Notes

Yesteryear

*"I have swept away your offenses like a cloud,
your sins like the morning mist. Return to me,
for I have redeemed you." -Isaiah 44:22*

*"I have been crucified with Christ and I no longer live, but
Christ lives in me. The life I now live in the body, I live by faith
in the Son of God, who loved me and gave himself for me."
-Galatians 2:20*

There are parts of my past I'm not proud of. There are also parts of my past that are very painful—things I had absolutely no control over at the time and would have never chosen to be a part of my story. Everyone has a past. In a way it has formed us into the people we are today, for better or for worse. There are two things about our past that I want to address. First, our past does not define us. Second, we determine what we do with it. Yes, it happened either to us or as a circumstance of our own choices, but our past is not who we are currently. Phew, praise the Lord! Amen?

We need to know where we've been to understand who we are. We need to understand who and where we are in order to move forward and grow. Dwelling in the past stunts us from being future focused. At the same time, looking into the future with no consideration to where we've been makes for shallow growth. We have the power to choose how our past affects us in the here and now. Is it going to cripple you with fear and anxiety? Is it going to make you feel guilt and shame that prevents you from growing? OR, is it going to refine you and grow you in ways you never knew?

This growth and refinement I'm talking about is not something we muster up the strength to do. It's all Him. He refines us, chiseling away all the ugly parts like a piece of stone on its way to becoming a masterpiece. He sees that ugly in our past and isn't turned away. Rather He draws near and says, "I can work with this. Together we are going to make beauty from ashes." Most of the prominent characters of the Bible had awful pasts. They were healed from it, they learned from it, and they went on to do amazing things for the kingdom. Can you give me one reason why you shouldn't do the same? God wrote greatness over you from the beginning, when He knew the mistakes you'd make and the ways you would fall short. Yet, that's still the plan—greatness, righteousness, holiness. For YOU...in YOU!

Pray with me: Lord, thank you that you are a God of healing and new beginnings. Thank you that you died for us while we were still sinners and that you care enough about us to turn our painful pasts into beautiful futures. Help me to trust you in the refining process. I know it's not going to be easy, but keep my eyes on you as you mold me into the woman you created me to be (past and all). Help me to be open to using my past to relate to other women and draw them near to you. I will repeat with my mouth until I believe with my mind that you have great things for me. Amen!

Notes

You Mean I Have to Tell People?

"Therefore, go and make disciples of all nations, baptizing them in the name of the Father and of the Son and of the Holy Spirit, and teaching them to obey everything I have commanded you. And surely, I am with you always, to the very end of the age." -Matthew 28:19-20

"When we live in fear to protect our name, we fail to live to proclaim His." -Lori McDaniel

The other day I was asking myself some hard questions. How concerned am I with aligning the way I live my life to what the Bible says my purpose is? Do I truly believe what the Bible says about my purpose? Maybe that seems like a less exciting part of the word that I'd like to sort of breeze over. As if I'm saying, "Give me all the blessings and the peace and the strength, God, but I'm going to just go ahead and use these things how I want to use them." Or maybe I'm striving to live a life pleasing to God, but the whole part about sharing it isn't as desirable? These were some sobering thoughts for sure and I encourage you to ask yourself the same questions.

In Matthew 28, Jesus had just resurrected and appeared first to the women (Mary and Mary Magdalene) and then to His disciples. In realizing that Jesus is actually there with them, the disciples fall down in worship. Then Jesus lays out the next steps— The Great Commission. He commands them to make disciples and to teach people about Him. What does this mean for us so many years later? It means the same exact thing; Jesus wants us to reach people with the truth about Him. It means living a life that resembles Christ's character. It means building relationships with those who don't know Him in order to walk life with them and point them toward Jesus. It means living beyond ourselves and lifting one another up so that we might glorify the Lord with our thoughts and words and actions. It means being honest and open with our struggles and about how God has redeemed those things in order to grow us and others.

Evangelism can sound scary and I know plenty of Christians who are turned off by it. I think there is a stigma about it because we've seen people do it poorly or falsely. Humans are bound to mess things up and twist something that is good and right to seem weird or undesirable. If we are reading the Bible for ourselves and truly believing that this was exactly what Jesus wanted us to do, then there's no question as to what our purpose is. We have to search our hearts and ask for guidance in how this plays out in our own lives.

In my life personally, it's praying and asking God to show me who in my day to day needs to feel His love. It's asking for Him to make me aware of the needs around me so that I don't miss opportunities to minister to the hearts I am surrounded by every day. It's teaching my kids about apologizing and forgiveness. It's also living in a state of transparency on social media, where people can take a look at my life and see that I am just a broken person in so much need of grace, and somehow through the mess God is doing something great with me. That's what evangelism looks like for me in this season. What does it look like for you?

Pray with me: *Jesus, thank you for dying for me. The greatness of your sacrifice is not lost on me. Let the joy of my salvation lead me to share your love and grace with others. Show me what that looks like in my day-to-day life during this season. Give me boldness to encourage and speak life in others. You are my purpose. You are my hope. Amen.*

Notes

Notes

Chapter 5: Are You a Joy Girl?
1. Kay Warren, *Choose Joy: Because Happiness Isn't Enough* (Grand Rapids, MI: Revell, 2013), 32.

Chapter 7: Boundaries
1. Dr. Henry Cloud & John Townsend, *Boundaries: When to Say Yes, How to Say No to Take Control of Your Life* (Grand Rapids, MI: Harper Collins Publishing, 1992), 45.

Chapter 15: Reluctance
1. Jessica Honegger, *Imperfect Courage* (Colorado Springs, CO: Waterbrook, 2018), 7.

Chapter 20: Anxious for Nothing
1. "Facts and Statistics," Anxiety and Depression Association of America, accessed November 2018, https://adaa.org/about-adaa/press-room/facts-statistics.

Chapter 22: Identity
1. Lysa TerKeurst, *Uninvited: Living Loved When You Feel Less Than, Left Out, and Lonely* (Nashville, TN: Nelson Books, 2016), 126.

Chapter 25: Inexhaustible
1. "Charles H. Spurgeon Quote," Quote Fancy, accessed August 2018, https://quotefancy.com/quote/785786/Charles-H-Spurgeon-If-Christ-were-only-a-cistern-we-might-soon-exhaust-his-fullness-but.

Chapter 36: Peace
1. "Awakening Quotes," Daily Inspirational Quotes, accessed August 2018, https://www.dailyinspirationalquotes.in/2017/02/peace-not-mean-place-no-noise-trouble-hard-work-means-midst-things-still-calm-heart/.

Chapter 42: The Three Letter Word
1. Lysa TerKeurst, *The Best Yes: Making Wise Decisions in the Midst of Endless Demands* (Nashville, TN: Nelson Books, 2014), 6.

Chapter 45: The Words We Say
1. Gary Chapman, The Five Love Languages (Chicago, IL: Northfield Publishing, 1992).

Chapter 50: You Mean I Have to Tell People?
1. "First Mission Trip Fears," Lori McDaniel Blog, accessed August 2018, http://www.lorimcdaniel.org/blog/.

Printed in the United States
By Bookmasters